MW01225454

IN THE FLESH

in the flesh

TWENTY WRITERS EXPLORE THE BODY
Edited by **Kathy Page** and **Lynne Van Luven**

BRINDLE
& GLASS

Copyright © 2012 Kathy Page and Lynne Van Luven

All rights reserved. No part of this publication may be reproduced, stored in
a retrieval system, or transmitted in any form or by any means—electronic,
mechanical, recording, or otherwise—without the prior written consent
of the publisher or a licence from The Canadian Copyright Licensing Agency
(ACCESS Copyright). For a copyright licence, visit accesscopyright.ca.

Brindle & Glass Publishing Ltd.
brindleandglass.com

LIBRARY AND ARCHIVES CANADA CATALOGUING IN PUBLICATION
In the flesh : twenty writers explore the body /
Kathy Page, Lynne Van Luven, editors.

Also issued in electronic format.
ISBN 978-1-926972-37-4

1. Canadian essays (English)—21st century. 2. Human body.
3. Body image. I. Page, Kathy, 1958– II. Van Luven, Lynne

PS8367.B63I5 2012   C814'.60803561   C2011-907343-9

Editor: Heather Sangster, Strong Finish
Design: Pete Kohut
Cover image: *Hugging* (detail), painting by Pete Kohut

Brindle & Glass is pleased to acknowledge the financial support for its publishing
program from the Government of Canada through the Canada Book Fund, Canada
Council for the Arts, and the Province of British Columbia through the British
Columbia Arts Council and the Book Publishing Tax Credit.

The interior pages of this book have been printed on 100% post-consumer
recycled paper, processed chlorine free, and printed with vegetable-based inks.

1 2 3 4 5 16 15 14 13 12

PRINTED IN CANADA

For our parents and families.

contents

Introduction: Prison and Paradise

Kathy Page and Lynne Van Luven

O, that this too solid flesh would melt
Thaw and resolve itself into a dew!
—Shakespeare, *Hamlet*, Act 1, Scene 2

Human beings have always had complex—even tormented—relationships with their own bodies. Unlike animals, we seem never fully at one with our flesh: we are either too much invested in or too little satisfied with our corporeal selves. And humans' conversations about (and with) their bodies have been going on for millennia. Plato saw the body as the "prison of the senses," and many since have followed suit. Writer Susie Orbach insists that "bodies are and always have been shaped according to the specific cultural moment. There has never been a 'natural' body." Sociologist Arthur Frank observes that "the body is not mute, but it is inarticulate. It does not use speech, yet begets it."

Some see the body as a machine, others as a mystery, "the thing-we-not-quite-are," according to philosopher Raymond Tallis. Some of us revel in our bodies and those of others. Walt Whitman wrote, "If any thing is sacred, the human body is sacred." However, just as many, if not more, of us regard our bodies as burdens or enemies of our well-being. Small wonder, perhaps, given what they let us in for. As David Abram puts it in *Becoming Animal*:

> To identify with the sheer physicality of one's flesh may well seem lunatic. The body is an imperfect and

1

breakable entity vulnerable to a thousand and one insults—to scars, and the scorn of others, to disease, decay, and death.

And yet, this is what we asked our authors to do. Choose a body part, we said, consider your relationship with it. Tell the truth. Be personal. Don't hold back . . .

The idea for *In the Flesh* simmered for a decade or so and underwent several quite violent metamorphoses before evolving into this particular form: twenty authors, each writing in a frank, personal way about a particular body part, thus creating a collective portrait of the human body in all its glory and squalor. Beset ourselves with our own human bodies, nowhere near cyborg strength, we nevertheless sent out emails far and wide. As the book took shape and our inboxes began to bristle with body parts, we realized we had implicated ourselves in a wonderfully suggestive narrative:

Trevor's eyes back to you
My vagina
Re: Penis 2
Sue's pancreas
Blood?
Sending you my breasts
The ear again
The RIGHT brain file
Re: Feelings about hair
Re: vagina/penis
Re: penis thoughts
Tai's skin

The momentum was irresistible. We had entered a thicket of double entendre and punning from which it seemed we might never emerge

(I have gone through Lorna C's brain with her twice and am ready to send it on to you... Caroline's hair is lovely... Please give us your tongue... We would be delighted for you to explore the female genitals... We know they/it will be in good hands... Re: Penis, if you need an extension, that's perfectly fine. Just tell us how long...).

This was okay, we told ourselves, quelling the giggles, wiping our eyes. Reactions to the body have ever oscillated from the sublime to the ridiculous, from the pure lines of Venus de Milo to the silly innuendo of Chuck Berry's "My Ding-a-ling." Even though the creation of *In the Flesh* has been a wild, convoluted, sometimes hilarious, always fascinating journey, it began straightforwardly enough. It sprang from a question, prompted by one of those sentences that seems to leap, by virtue of deceptive simplicity and outright oddness, from the page of Klaus Theweleit's book *Male Fantasies*: "Historians have never been interested in what has really happened to human bodies—what bodies have felt." True, of course. History concerns itself with thoughts and deeds, trade, war, the law, and, at most, living conditions and average lifespans. So what do our bodies feel now? And how do we experience our bodies, or parts of them?

Once inhibitions fall away, almost everyone engages in body talk. (Like the raunchy character in Chaucer's "The Wife of Bath's Tale," we enjoy being bawdy.) Our motives include base curiosity and even voyeurism, but they go beyond that. In these increasingly virtual, postmodern times, it sometimes seems as if we're chronicling a relationship about to change beyond recognition, or even vanish. We live at a time when former science-fiction fantasies are part of our daily reality. Our physicality, already transformed by the industrial and post-industrial revolutions, is further altered by the operating theatre and the laboratory. Transplantation, for example, is now an established element in the medical repertoire—and has led to both incredibly altruistic and terribly base human behaviours. The human genome is being decoded; we can know, with varying degrees of certainty, our medical futures and have begun to debate the possibilities and ethical dilemmas of genetic engineering, hybridizing and cloning.

Our concepts of identity, bodily integrity, and even of what constitutes humanness are thrown into relief, and they may be forced to evolve rapidly. As Susie Orbach suggests in her book *Bodies*, we are living at a time when, bombarded with idealized imagery, the bodies of those living in affluent countries generate ongoing anxiety, an ethical jungle, huge amounts of commerce, and vast amounts of work. She sees us as standing on the cusp of a new era "between a post-industrial moment and a time when bodies will be precision bio-engineered" and urges us to do what we can to make peace with our flesh.

Nevertheless, despite the ever-increasing barrage of information about our bodies, they remain a mystery to us, or perhaps a paradox. Chromosomes, hormones, cells, bone, cartilage, electrical impulses—all consort inside us. The body is us—and not us. We are in a process of continuous transformation: we have been embryos, children, young women or men, pregnant, thin, fat, sick, better again. We may not notice it but we are always changing—moving toward death, a point at which our cells and organs will stop functioning. All this internal process, of which we are mostly unaware, happens involuntarily.

But always and inevitably, the body does flex its muscle: in times of acute awareness of the flesh—pleasure and pain, sudden incapacities, injuries, the extremities of pregnancy, birth—we suddenly live right in our bodies. When we are *all* body and filled with a sense of horror, amazement, ecstasy, then we are forced to have a relationship with the silent partner, the one we ignore but finally can't avoid, the entity that makes everything possible and sets our limits too. This book, we hope, will offer readers another such experience: a journey, via the word and the intellect, back to the flesh we are made from.

We had only twenty parts to assign; consequently, *In the Flesh* is the result of a combination of editorial encouragement and authorial choice. Naturally enough, contributors' various bodily events intervened during the writing process. Consequently, the body portrayed in these pages is incomplete. These gaps bothered us a great deal to begin with; we had desperately wanted to create an enormous, encyclopedic book that encompassed even the toenail and the appendix. In the spirit of Andrew Marvell, who, in his poem "To His Coy Mistress," wished for "an age at least to every part," we felt we needed an essay on the nipple, another on the bellybutton, or the vas deferens. All parts deserve attention: after all, did not Charlotte Roche recently pen an entire novel in which the heroine's anus was a major character? How then could we possibly offer this book to readers without an essay on the lungs, which keep the whole show going, something about DNA, a mention, at least, of the thyroid? And what of the ribs?

Yet, as the contributions continued, we began to see the non-standard nature of our emerging body in a positive light; one of the wonders of the human body is its sheer adaptability. The double-gendered body in these pages is no Adonis or Diana, but it has a heart, brain, hands, some innards, limber legs, and a lovely head of hair; it can see, hear, touch, lust, reproduce, feel, and think. We'll have to assume the lungs, since it has a tongue and can speak.

face,
hair,
tongue . . .

Reading Faces
Julian Gunn

The way in which the other presents himself, exceeding the
idea of the other in me, we here name face.
—Emmanuel Levinas, *Totality and Infinity*

I'm having my head scanned for science. For forensic anthropology, in particular. It turns out you don't have to be dead to be of
use to a forensic anthropologist. A scanner originally designed to
analyze automobile parts is a few inches from my closed eyelids,
and a red laser shines on my forehead. This scanner's name is
Scorpion, and its shape is, in fact, vaguely reminiscent of a pair of
claws outstretched to clasp my face. The scorpion's tail is attached
to various apparati, including a laptop computer, all arranged on
my kitchen counter.

Stenton MacKenzie is in town, which means interesting things
are going to happen. Stenton's an old friend of mine. He's a PHD
student in forensic anthropology—the kind who exports his
motorcycle from Canada to Dundee, Scotland, because getting
to know the landscape, its topography, is an integral part of his
education. He also took along the bones of his beloved dachshund,
Bobo, but those were a study tool. Stenton is analyzing the faces of
transmen—people born female who identify as male—who have
taken testosterone, the hormone prescribed for masculinization.
He is investigating whether facial bone structure is altered by
the use of the hormone. Very little is known about the long-term
effects of testosterone use. We know that taking testosterone bulks

up the facial musculature. Stenton believes that it also alters the bone structure. Beyond that, he believes that transpeople need to have a presence in science, as researchers and subjects—a "human face." So, on this working visit back in Victoria, he's the researcher and I'm the subject.

Right now, he is having trouble scanning my face. The Scorpion produces a 3D model of a surface, which Stenton exports to other visualizing software. He superimposes the post-testosterone 3D facial model on a pre-testosterone photograph to compare the face over time. A CAT scan would be better, but that's not permitted for non-medical research. And the equipment wouldn't fit in his suitcase.

The Scorpion is reliably fussy, so a number of things could be wrong. It rejects shiny surfaces, but we've determined through a tissue test that my face isn't greasy—that is, I wiped it with a tissue. The problem may be the lighting. Even on a dark day like this, Canada just can't duplicate the pervasive gloom of a Scottish winter, so my skylights may be interfering. The scanner also doesn't like metal, and I have a small titanium patch in my neck where two vertebrae were surgically fused.

I sit quietly, with my eyes shut. "Your blink reflex is so fast," Stenton reassures me, "that even if you did look into the laser, you almost certainly wouldn't be blinded." He grins to let me know he's joking. "There's almost no risk to your vision." It's not unlike going to the dentist. I am gifted with weak teeth, so I know how to sit quietly while people do odd things to my face. I have already had to make certain sacrifices for research. The scanner can't deal with facial hair, so this morning I shaved off my goatee. It's something of a blow to my vanity, but the idea of being studied wins out. I want to discover what can be known about me by looking at my face.

I'm not alone. Faces are a big deal right now. Recent neurological research has generated popular interest in face recognition. On radio shows and podcasts such as the amazing Radiolab, the phenomenon of prosopagnosia, or the inability to recognize faces, has been under discussion. Celebrated neurologist Oliver Sacks recently revealed his own severe face blindness. This fascinates me. A scientist whose writing shows a profound gift for recognizing the humanity of a patient is unable to identify the same patient on sight. Sacks is especially good at understanding the way that a medical symptom and a personality can be intertwined—productively, problematically, even poetically. Sacks has made a case study of himself, calling into question what it means to perceive another human being. Now I'm trying to become a case study myself, but my own medical problem may be complicating things.

In addition to having provided the wrong kind of light and possibly the wrong kind of neck, I'm worrying about Stenton's scan because I am having a Puffy Day. I have a condition called angioedema. It's not as bad as the Latin and Greek mixture of its name makes it sound. It isn't edema of the heart, for example. It's more like hives. Under stressful situations and in response to some allergens, angioedema causes my face, hands, and feet to swell up with histamine. This was revealed to me through my old nemesis, dentistry. Angioedema often manifests as a reaction to dental work or other stressful situations, such as being in graduate school (like Stenton, I'm a grad student, an English MA) or having a laser pointed at your face. Angioedema can be seriously disfiguring for people with severe cases, and it can also be life-threatening if the airway swells shut. My dentist became much less excited about finishing off my root canal when I told him about the remote possibility of my dying in the chair. I still have a bright blue temporary filling in the back of my mouth.

I'm lucky. My swelling is relatively minor. Most noticeably, the area on either side of my mouth swells up. This can push my lips forward into a fish pout or make the contours around my mouth disappear. My upper lip may puff up and jut out. My cheeks can feel like slabs of gelatin. My hands don't swell up in an obvious way, but their skin takes on the same strange, thick texture, and they hurt, the pressure in each phalanx of the finger making it into a sore little balloon that can't expand. I grow the goatee, now sacrificed to the Scorpion, and often cultivate a rugged two- or three-(or six-) day growth of stubble to disguise the distortion when I look in the mirror.

When I'm having an attack, as I have been more or less continuously for a year, my face becomes subtly estranged. There's a popular term to describe the feeling of looking at computer animation when the image is good but not good enough to be convincing (for example, the way the faces seem frozen, like speaking masks): the uncanny valley. Looking at my puffy face in the mirror produces a similar kind of unease in me. It looks like an imperfect, yet unarguably accurate, replica. The things I like about my face, the gestures and expressions I think of as mine, look like caricatures performed by a stiff-faced replica.

Yet most of my friends tell me they don't notice. I should be reassured, but I find it perversely distressing. We count on other people to reflect us back to ourselves. It's a little akin to the indignation I feel when my photo software's face-recognition utility identifies someone else's face as mine. I may grudgingly acknowledge some resemblance, but I feel as though the computer has failed to recognize precisely the subtle qualities that make my face mine—the *me* of my face. The me of my face is not the way I resemble other people, but the way in which my face is unique. (Admittedly, it was a blurry photo, and we were both wearing toques.)

Of course, I could be indignant only once I noticed that all of my photo applications had suddenly started recognizing faces. They were rapidly getting better at it. I also began to notice mention of defence research in articles and podcasts about face recognition. It turns out that the current collective interest in faces is not entirely motivated by scientific curiosity and aesthetic delight. Your photo app's power to recognize your face so well is a side effect of the desire of governments and military organizations to be able to use computers to recognize people at a distance, from grainy footage, at strange angles, in poor light. The human brain can do it in seconds. Surveillance experts and military leaders want a scanner to do it.

Stenton and I want the Scorpion to do it too, but the machine won't co-operate. I'm released from my blind immobility to aid in the investigation. We try scanning an empty margarine container: it works fine. We try a butternut squash I've been meaning to roast for ages. Flawless. We scan the underside of my forearm. A clear, if alarmingly textured, surface appears on the screen. We try my face again. Nothing. We can't get a stable image. I feel unsettled. Without a scan, my face can't be part of the research, and I'm surprised at how disappointed I feel.

Clearly it is time for a pint. We adjourn to the corner pub. Once, on a drinking expedition like this, we compared scars, and naturally Stenton won. All I had for public display were some feeble scrapes from bicycling accidents and the very faint scar across my throat where the surgeons went in to fuse my spine. When it came to Stenton's turn, he showed me a kind of portmanteau scar. He could pull the skin of his eyelid almost an inch away from his eye in a genuinely alarming way—the result of a serious car accident.

Stenton is not working on face recognition for the military-industrial complex, which is something of a relief. I've asked him what drew him to study faces. "They're the most important part of the evolutionary kit that we have, next to the brain." I wanted to know what he thinks about in his professional capacity when he looks at a face. "The 'forensic' in forensic anthropology is always about identifying ethnicity, age, and sex. I find myself automatically trying to look through the superficial layers of soft tissue to the bone structures." He lists off a number of technical terms I have trouble keeping in order: zygomatics (cheekbones), prognathism (forward projection), superior orbital ridge (under the eyebrows), bossing (forehead angle).

He has projections of his research results. "I expect the greatest changes will occur in the mandible,"—meaning the jaw—"the zygomatics, and possibly the brow ridges. Or not." This matches my experience of taking testosterone. My jaw filled out, or became more "rugose," as Stenton puts it. I can't say whether or not my eyebrow ridges protrude more than they used to, because my eyebrows got shaggy enough to hide any subtle changes. As time passes, they creep alarmingly closer to a unibrow.

Sex, surprisingly, is not that easy to determine in a skull. "There are specific morphological and morphometric signatures in features which will 'weight' a skull more toward male or female," he writes. "Ethnicity is a factor. For example, Dutch females tend to have relatively rugose mandibles and large crania, which in isolation could lead you to think their skull was male. Sexing and assessing ethnicity is all about balancing several factors in relation to each other to come to the most accurate estimation." And all this is part of the process of identifying the dead: who they were, what happened to them, how they died.

How they lived too. It was strange looking through a series of before and after photos of transmen with Stenton. Though we are both transmen ourselves, our reactions were quite different. I was amazed by how similar each face was before and after, and yet how transformed it seemed in terms of whether I read it as male or female. In contrast, Stenton looked at a face and then tried to see through the face. He was convinced that the underlying structure must have changed. He says that when he looks at a skull he imagines both what's behind and what's overlaid: the contours of the human brain and the topography of the human face.

And this is a man who knows heads. My friend has led many lives. In one of them, he worked as a hairdresser in a small Vancouver Island village. "Those years behind the hairdressing chair," he told me, "really did leave me with a 'feel' for heads and faces, without my ever being aware of it until I started studying facial anthropology."

The face is everything, in a way. "Face" as a gestalt is so wired into our brains that we see faces everywhere. We see them in grainy photos of Mars. We make car headlights and grilles into faces. We can even see a face in an iconic grouping of a circle, two dots and an arc, or, as in early emoticons, a colon and a parenthesis looked at sideways: :). Emoticons themselves developed because without seeing an expression and hearing a tone of voice we can't read each other's meaning properly. We fall into default assumptions of hostility and endless semantic wrangling, as you will know if you've ever been involved in even a minor argument over the Internet.

This almost happened between Stenton and me while we were planning for his visit. We got into a near-argument about whether he should use Facebook to advertise for participants. Even the name was apt. He feared he might breach the university regulations managing ethics and copyright. I wanted to use the social media capacity to reach more potential subjects. I thought he was being officious, and he found me defensive and snappish. Now, seeing his face, able to read his expressions, I know his gentleness, and he knows that I know. It's in my face.

We debate whether or not to try the scan again. Stenton has other faces to collect. He's made appointments with subjects in other cities. Rather than frustrate ourselves now, we decide to try again when he comes back through town. When he does return, a few weeks later, it's to tell me ruefully that the scanner is acting up everywhere. He hasn't been able to collect a single face. I feel selfishly relieved. At least there isn't something strange about my face in particular. It isn't out of phase with the rest of reality. I'm not a vampire.

Instead of science, we turn to another area of his expertise. He introduces me to "black velvet," a mixture of champagne and Guinness. It is a surprisingly graceful way to get both down at once. We drink a number of these and talk about our own faces.

"I feel like a blob of dough with two little eyes stuck in it," I say.

"My ears stick out," Stenton says generously. "I have an enormous nose, and I'm bald. At least you have your hair."

A little later, walking only slightly more slowly than usual into the bathroom, I find that alcohol has done its usual work on my perceptual apparatus and made me noticeably more attractive. Stenton tells me that we are hard-wired to prefer symmetrical faces. In fact, symmetry is one of the markers we used to identify people. The angioedema is often asymmetrical, which adds to my self-consciousness. The hardest thing to deal with is not the change in my face, it's the mutability. From hour to hour, day to day, I do not know what part of my face will be swollen and what part will be normal. I don't know how long it will last, and I can make only educated guesses about what causes it. Most of the time the triggers of angioedema are obscure. A face is always a story through time as well as an expressive and receptive surface in motion, a space. How do I, like Oliver Sacks, accommodate my disease? How does it become not just part of my self-image, but part of my way of being in the world?

A similar question applies to all of us as we get older. Age is the force that impels a change in our relationship to our faces. Stenton and I are both relatively elderly for graduate students. I'm thirty-seven, and he's approaching fifty. In our background discussion via email, Stenton explained about evaluating age forensically. "Age is something you can approximate in the living and in a cadaver, as long as the face is not destroyed or decayed beyond assessment criteria," he wrote. "You do it according to written guidelines and your own intuition, which comes to us courtesy of accrued, largely unconscious, general social knowledge. There are some studies which document that people are better at estimating the age of someone in their own bracket." I notice this in my department at the university. Most of the other MA students are in their mid-twenties, and they do tend to underestimate my age (bless them). I can see the difference. The bloom of youth is more than a cliché. In some lights their faces seem as radiant as lanterns. Next to theirs, my skin looks like slightly over-thumbed paperwork. Yet the angioedema has some genuinely strange effects. You can imagine from my description that it acts a little like a collagen injection. It smoothes out wrinkles and plumps out my cheeks. In some ways it seems to reverse the effects of aging. Sometimes I look younger when I'm having an attack, but then the condition also emphasizes the horizontal wrinkles in my forehead, so that I look like a very worried, round-faced child—in short, like Charlie Brown.

Our skulls, too, change as we age. "In terms of bone," Stenton says, "age is primarily determined by the teeth, if they're present,"—in which case my temporary filling would be useful—"the degree of resorption of mandibular and maxillae bone, and also by the degree of fusion of cranial sutures." The process of transformation is unceasing. My grandmother is in her mid-eighties now, and in the last few years a startling change has come over her face. She has moved out of the usual depredations of aging into a new, strange beauty. Her skin is so delicate that the veins and arteries show as a blue and pink iridescence that reminds me of abalone. The whites of her eyes are stained like the imperfections in quartz. There is something translucent about her, as though she were only a projection of herself, as though she were already moving elsewhere—this image just the glow that remained of her, like the light of a receding star.

We mix more drinks and talk about work. I'm a teaching assistant. I mark papers and explain the proper use of commas. Back in Dundee, Stenton works as a lab assistant in his department, a considerably messier proposition. I've asked him how his students feel about facial dissections. Stenton always speaks of the dissection room with a certain relish. "The students really balk when they get to the face. Most of the time, when they're working on the body, they keep the head and face covered with a cloth. At decapitation time, we demonstrators step in. It's a surprisingly aggressive task. Last year I was right up on the trolleys, trying to get a purchase, and ended up having to do a fair bit of wrenching. Students were appalled." For all his ghoulish delight, I know that, like Oliver Sacks, Stenton has a profound appreciation for the humanity of other people. Exploring the structure of the face, intimately, through its layers, to the bone beneath, is another way to understand what it is to be human.

Forensic anthropology isn't all yanking the heads off cadavers. "I'm sometimes given facial comparison tasks. That may mean doing an analysis between photographs, sculptures and paintings to try to sort out the authenticity of an identity in portraiture." As background to our discussion, he showed me a study he had participated in. The goal was to evaluate whether an 1886 Jeanne Donnadieu pastel was a portrait of Vincent van Gogh. Stenton also sent me a book chapter he'd contributed to titled "Facial Identification of the Dead," which, although it sounded to me like the title of an edgy independent film, he assured me was "dreadfully boring."

Stenton and I never do manage to make the scanner work on my face. "Never mind, chum," he says. "The beard will grow back."

Philosopher Emmanuel Levinas writes about the profound mutual effect of human presence. We are accustomed to think that other people inspire competition and fear, that we have an innate response of hostility. Levinas tells us that the presence of another person gives rise to an infinite sense of compassion and responsibility. He calls this interaction "the face," though what he means by the face goes beyond the visual to an encounter with another's spirit or soul. Or perhaps it is something like the proprioceptive response to another human's proximity, if you want to get speculative. Meeting another person exceeds all our ideas of that person, and we are overwhelmed and humbled by their presence.

Because of this power of the face, it seems strange to me that the gift for recognizing each other, this primary act of human connection, should be put in train to recognize an *enemy*. This is at least one goal of face-recognition software modelled on human perception. We may soon be able to build a scanner that will scan my face through a goatee, a scanner that will measure the bone density of a transperson's skull, or a scanner that will recognize a fugitive's face in darkness, at an oblique angle, half-turned away from the camera that was noticed too late. When everyone's face can be identified everywhere we go, will we think to be curious about how we recognize—or fail to recognize—the humanity of these faces?

Stenton tends to arrive and depart abruptly. A few days after the failed scanning mission, he's back in Dundee, leaving me with a full bottle of leftover champagne. His visits are the bright spots in my slog through graduate school, my twenty-four-hour leave from trying to be a responsible citizen. When he has gone, I look at my face in the mirror. The alcohol will probably exacerbate the angio. Still, right now I look tired but not unhappy. Something heavy in my expression has lifted, some indefinable tension in the tiny muscles has relaxed. We have that effect on each other. He relaxes my tension, and I soothe his sometimes frenzied energy. I wonder again, as I do occasionally, why we have never been lovers. Some chemical catalyst that failed to show up at the appointed moment? My reflexive timidity coupled with the fact that he drives like a madman? In a way, it doesn't matter. I know that we have seen and recognized each other's faces—not just the aging, testosterone-inflected, scarred, or weary surfaces that clothe these skulls. What we have seen is each other's humanity, the thing in each of us that meets and embraces even when we are on different continents, embarked on different journeys, even if we never see each other's face again.

120,000 Strands

Caroline Adderson

A heart-shaped chocolate box, paisley-patterned in hot pink. Very 1970s. By the look of its crushed cloth bow, the box has been around since then. It's been around in various trunks and closets of wide-ranging addresses—from my childhood room in Sherwood Park, Alberta, to Vancouver, to New Orleans and Toronto, then back to Vancouver. For thirty-seven years I've kept this box and its contents with me.

In early photographs I have a blond pixie cut, often with Who of Whoville-like feelers sticking up. By the time I was six, someone, probably me, decided to grow my hair long. I can't recall the intermediate-length years, just me the Pixie, then me with two ratty braids hanging down from the Montreal Expos cap, the ends secured with bauble fasteners.

At first my mother did my braids. (She would occasionally put my hair in rags too, which I loved because, unragged the next morning, my boringly straight hair would bounce with Bo Peep ringlets.) Every morning before school she braided—expertly, thanklessly—until the day she announced she'd had enough. Probably the shrieking that accompanied the preliminary combing made her up and quit. She said I had to learn myself. "Watch," she said. Over, under, over, under. Her hands moved in the mirror; mine mimicked them on the other side. Easy. Braiding is one of those things you learn by doing. Thinking about it, breaking it down into steps, actually makes it harder, like driving a car with a standard transmission, like dancing the salsa.

I had been braiding my own hair for some time when I entered my Brownie phase. Friends of mine had already joined, and soon I, too, yearned to peddle cookies door to door in the brown uniform. (I probably thought I'd get to keep the money.) The badges were a further draw. Long-time Brownies had so many badges that the orange of their sashes barely showed. And while some would have to be hard-earned (Astronomer, Bannock Maker), others I could have immediately, with barely any effort, as easily as I collected the china animal figurines from Red Rose tea.

We met in the gym at Salisbury Composite High School in Sherwood Park, the Tweenies, those aspiring Brownies who had not yet been pledged, separated from the proven Brownies. After some tedious speeches and singing, we were set free to start earning our badges at various stations set up around the room. I went directly to the braiding station, where three old nylon stockings were tied to the back of a chair. Brown Owl stood by watching me. Picture Brown Owl if you can: clipboard, little moustache, appropriately gigantic glasses. I made short work of those nylons. I whipped them into a braid so fast Brown Owl could not help but let out a hoot of astonishment.

The badges were right there, fixed to her clipboard. Why I even remember this years and years later is because, despite my clearly demonstrated virtuoso ability, she wouldn't give me one!

"It's backward," she sniffed.

I tried again. I tried at least three times, but I'd learned to braid in the mirror. I couldn't reverse the way my hands moved and do it the way Brown Owl wanted. Finally, she lost patience and sent me off to try my luck at some other station.

Weeks later, when I had finally processed the real meaning of this incident, I quit Brownies in protest, the very day I was pledged, in fact. That first evening, though, I did what Brown Owl told me to do. I marched away, fuming and sputtering, my notion of injustice awakened for the first time, brown shoes kicking against all the pettiness that awaited me in the adult world.

The box is quite heavy, though not as heavy as a box of chocolates. Still, the weight of it is a surprise once you find out what's inside. Some very creased crêpe paper and, nestled in that, a coil of hair.

Two years before we got married, my husband-to-be came down with a headache. We were with his parents at their cabin on an island off the Sechelt Peninsula in British Columbia. He took his pain to bed, and two days later both were still there. In fact, his headache was worse. He was nauseated by it now and needed a doctor.

We drove straight to the ferry, then to Emergency in Vancouver, and after many agonizing hours, my husband-to-be was seen. It seemed he had a migraine.

"Can a thirty-five-year-old with absolutely no history of migraines suddenly come down with one?" I asked.

They said yes, but they would do a CAT scan just to be sure.

Here came the biggest mistake I'd ever made in my life. My husband was then a struggling film student. He subsisted mostly on eggs and beer, and one of the ways he cut back on expenses was not paying his Medical Service Plan premiums. When they offered the CAT scan, the first thing I thought was how much it would cost him. Besides, here he was, sitting up in the hospital bed attached to an IV, pumped full of some migraine miracle. He was smiling, his pain-free self again.

We left without the CAT scan.

Within twenty-four hours the headache came back double-strength, then triple. He couldn't eat or tolerate any light. I took him back to Emergency. Again, they claimed he had a migraine and gave him an IV, which once again seemed to work, at least while we were there. I had paid his debt to MSP by then and signed him up again. Since he was fully insured now, I asked for the CAT scan. I pleaded for it. They said it was unnecessary.

For the next week, my husband lay in my darkened bedroom.

I would spoon-feed him. He would vomit in the pail. Two more trips to Emergency, two more CAT scans denied. Then one night he began saying peculiar things. He said Telefilm was trying to fax his electrocardiogram to him. Mere mention of the hospital made him roar out, his speech all slurry: "Don't throw me to the wolves!"

Wolves?

Wolves turned out to be the secret password that immediately gets you a CAT scan. In my husband's case, it showed a massive, rapidly growing brain tumour. They ran with him to the operating room, me trotting beside the stretcher. "I love you, I love you, I love you . . ." The doors swung closed in my face, and I was left to find my way back to the waiting area, alone and in shock from how fast things had happened after so many days of excruciating, underwater slowness.

But it wasn't a tumour. It was a hematoma—a huge blood clot growing in his brain. Wheeled out of post-op, he was all smiles, completely oblivious to the trauma we had just lived through. The next day he was sitting up in ICU reading *The Sound and the Fury*. The day after that he was walking. Five days after brain surgery, he came home.

At which time, *I* took to my bed. I couldn't explain to him how devastating the whole episode had been. I should have been happy he was alive and that he had made such an astonishing recovery, and I was. But for ten straight days I'd nursed a man who was essentially dying; the fact of it only now sank in—the game of chance we'd barely won. I was sickened by guilt. If he *had* died, it would have been my fault, because I had said no to that first CAT scan. I'd said no for the unworthiest of all reasons—*money*.

They'd shaved the back of his head for the operation, which had required a piece of his skull to be removed. Now he was scored with purple Frankenstein sutures. One night he visited a friend, an actress who had been in his student films. She owned a barber's shaver and offered to rid him of the old curls that still massed incongruously around his face.

I sobbed when I saw his shorn head. Again, my reaction per-plexed and frustrated him. "That was you," I told him. "That was your hair. Your *hair* is gone."

Three long, coppery brown hanks, each secured by an ordinary elastic, all three sections gathered into a ponytail with a paper bow off some long ago birthday present. Even now, decades later, the smell of Clairol Herbal Essences is heady.

In 1994, the year before my husband's hematoma, I read an article in *The New Yorker* about the room full of hair at the Auschwitz museum. I became so haunted by it that the room full of hair grew into the central image of my first novel. In order to write about it, I had to see it, and so I made the trip to Poland.

One of the most disturbing things about visiting Auschwitz today is that it looks almost picturesque. With its rows of two-storey brick barracks and lush green grass and trees, it seems more like meticulously maintained social housing than the twentieth century's primary locus of horror. There are photomurals, displays, films to watch, and the terrible sign above the gate, *Arbeit Macht Frei*, but it is still a modern museum with all the usual museum amenities, streaming with visitors and guided tour groups. To fathom the death camp it was and the horrors that happened there requires a huge imaginative leap.

To understand anything about Auschwitz, you must make certain connections. For example, Block 5 now houses "Material Evidence of Crimes." Among this evidence is a small hill of brushes in an almost empty room: nail brushes, shaving brushes, tooth brushes, lint brushes, shoe brushes, scrub brushes. Hair brushes.

In the hall outside the room hangs a photomural of the Everest of brushes from which this modest sample was taken. What you need to do even to come close to understanding Auchwitz is to connect the actual hair brushes inside the room to the thousands of confiscated hair brushes in the photomural in the hall, and in doing so grasp that each brush is more than an object, that it stands for the person who brought it here, perhaps in one of the battered brown leather suitcases you will shortly see displayed upstairs. You have to imagine that person packing her personal effects for this last trip, tucking in her brush, expecting to use it. Expecting to brush her hair again. Expecting to live long enough to. You have to imagine that small gesture, so imbued with hope.

Then move on to Block 4, where a sign in the doorway reads: *"The one who does not remember history is bound to live through it again."* This hall is lined with photographs of prisoners taken from three angles—profile, three-quarters, and face forward. All of them wear the striped jacket. Some have appliquéd symbols above their prison numbers—a triangle, a star. All have shaved heads. (Connection: First they take away the hair brushes, then they take away the hair.) How generic people look without their hair! Before I went to the Auschwitz museum, I had thought the opposite was the case because of the way certain celebrities are famous for being bald. But seen in a long gallery like the one in Block 4, face after face, it becomes obvious that features unframed by hair actually recede, much the way an unframed picture does. If you go to the Auschwitz museum and stand in the hall of Block 4, you might come to this same realization: that so much of our personality is expressed in our hair, which was the point of shaving the prisoners in the first place.

When my husband had his head shaved, he looked like a different person, but it was actually me who was different. He remembers nothing beyond the first few days of his headache. If he ever feared for his life, or resolved to become a better man when his suffering was over, he doesn't remember it. My reaction (an overreaction to him) was partly a result of trauma. But it was also because, the year before, I had stood in Block 4 of the Auschwitz museum where the prisoners' hair was collected and baled like straw and sold for thread, mattress stuffing, fuses for bombs, tailor's lining, and felt insulators for army boots, among other things. It seemed to me then (and now) that to have a part of your body taken from you and literally commodified was to be utterly negated as a human being. This is what I always think of when I see a shaved head, though he didn't know it.

He didn't know a shaved head reminds me of climbing to the second floor of Block 4. Of the chemical odour that pervades the air there, so strong it sticks in the back of the throat. It's some kind of preservative they use on the hair. For upstairs in Block 4 is the room full of hair I had come expressly to see.

The average human head holds 120,000 strands of hair. They grow from bulb-shaped follicles in the scalp's dermis. At the bottom of the follicle, soft precursor cells are nourished. They grow and divide and then, pushed upward by more cells growing beneath, they die. Hair, the very growing, shining, tangling thing that seems most alive about a person, each strand bearing the stuff of life, our DNA, is actually dead. How is it possible that these cells are dead when they seem so alive and expressive? In moments of terror, hair rises on the nape and arms; it falls out in grief or sorrow, or is torn out; it reflects our age and state of health, the ravages of cancer treatment. The way we style it tells much about the time in which we live, how we feel about ourselves, even our religion and our politics. Some people think that the hair in the Auschwitz museum, being human remains, should not even be on display. Yet how to comprehend the place—or try to—without the hair?

The room is about fifteen metres long with a wide floor-to-ceiling glass case along one wall. Inside it the hair is banked, higher at the back, tapering toward the glass, creating an avalanche effect. This is what you need to notice if you stand in that room: so many years have gone by that the hair in the case is balled up and matted. It looks like dull brown fleece. The astonishing array of colours human hair comes in, colours that change throughout a single life, from the shock of newborn black, to a toddler's white-blond (gradually darkening then rebleaching every summer), the dyes we use, then the grey when we give up, and finally, if we are lucky, the white—all of it has faded here. If you can complete the imaginative leap, if you can bear to make the final connections, you will understand that you are actually standing in a room with the twice-dead hair of *thousands* of the *millions* of people who suffered and perished in the camps and that their hair, too, is becoming dust, making it all the more imperative that you never, ever forget this place.

I stand at the mirror and hold my childhood hair against my head. My present hair looks unnatural, dark underneath, threaded with grey, the blond highlights chemically arranged on top. Strange how the old hair, the hair of my childhood, is young. It is lustrous and strong. This is the hair I learned to braid with, the hair I had when I first developed a sense of justice. Without a sense of justice, can we develop a conscience? Without a conscience, are we even human?

And it occurs to me that there is nothing else we treasure and hide away in trunks and closets that we can actually hold in our hands, that is ourselves at a different age, except for our hair and teeth. They outlast us, or so we hope. Stored in the heart-shaped chocolate box is something that was me. I hold it against my head. Here I am, before and after, then and now, my whole life in 120,000 strands.

Back into the paisley-patterned chocolate box it goes, tucked inside the wrinkled crêpe paper. Before I close the box, I take a marker and write inside the lid—a hope, a wish. *Remember me.*

The Tongue, from Childhood to Dotage

Madeleine Thien

We do not often think about our tongues. The tongue, I realized this morning, is the only organ that we bite accidentally, as if, in the darkened mouth, we forget where we have placed it, and we sometimes trip over it as one might trip over the leg of a table, even though we use that table every day of our lives.

Lately, I have been thinking a great deal about my tongue, which is visible and yet invisible to both intimates and strangers. The tongue, it is rumoured, was the last body part to be chosen for this anthology. It sat, gathering dust, while the penis, brain, heart, and breasts wobbled off in the hands of their proud owners. Despite its tensile musculature, its elaborate dance steps (eating and imbibing, speaking, lubricating, kissing, singing, pleasuring), its shy modesty, nobody was willing to speak for the tongue.

So it falls to me to tell you that the tongue is the mother of all body parts.

Not long ago, I came across the last words of composer Johannes Brahms, who, on his deathbed, asked for a glass of red wine. After sipping the liquid, he said, "That tastes nice. Thank you." Could I also, I wondered, leave this world with the taste of something beloved on my lips? "Thus, with a kiss, I die," wrote Shakespeare. Thus, Romeo entered the netherworld, carrying the memory of Juliet.

A dribble: the amount of saliva produced during the average Canadian lifetime is thirty thousand litres. Saliva, the motor oil of our bodies.

1. Childhood

Yes, the tongue is the mother of all organs. As babies, we gaze drunkenly into a kaleidoscope of shadows, we beat our little fists ineffectually, but our tongue boldly goes forth to meet the world. With this tiny, moist finger, we seek nourishment and protection, we seek love. We are ready to taste existence.

Give me sustenance! the tongue says. I am here at the centre of the world. And if you don't give me what I need, I will let you have it.

As a baby, I cried a great deal, apparently. My scrawny voice succeeded in alerting my parents to the fact that I was dying: I had been born with an extra half kidney that was poisoning my system. Months later, on my first birthday, the offending piece was cut away and removed. Every night in the hospital, my mother later told me, I hollered and wailed and fought. I despised my hospital crib. I tore my soft, pink blanket to bits. I shrieked until someone came to pick me up: and not just anyone. Only my father would do.

My father's language, Hakka, is foreign to me. The word itself, *hakka*, means the guest people, the ones who have left behind their homes and settled in a new land.

For a few years when my grandmother lived with us in Canada, I would hear the two of them speaking Hakka, but once she returned to Malaysia, I never heard my father speak the language again. In my memory, it is a whispered language, intoned with a mixture of anxiety and love, a worried noise, fearful of misunderstanding.

My mother's language, Cantonese, is referred to, disdainfully, as the language of the rickshaw drivers. It is a language for the sharp-tongued and the quick-witted, for people who need to run and shout, eat and sprint.

I was raised in English; it was my job to speak to authorities and to write letters and other official documents with my perfect English grammar. English is my mother tongue, and it is, in many ways, a gift my parents gave me, hoping that I would raise my voice inside this new world. Many nights during my childhood, my parents went off to their second or third jobs and left us at home. If the doorbell buzzed or the phone rang, my sister and I would drop to the carpet, covering our mouths with our hands. We had a vague, uneasy sense that the authorities were coming for us. Never, my parents said, should it pass our lips that we spent most of our time unsupervised. At the age of six, while trying to make dinner, I ignited a slice of bread in the toaster oven. (Both sides were coated so heavily with margarine that the bread exploded into a ball of flame.) Not long after, while deep-frying potatoes, I started an oil fire in the wok. But all was resolved, and neither my sister nor I breathed a word of the near disasters.

We kept all of our family secrets this way, lodged in the mind, hidden from the tongue.

An aside: Spices appeared in human cuisine as long as fifty thousand years ago and so began their migration to the corners of the world. The tongue, insatiable and salivating, was the harbinger of civilization.

My father, the kitchen magician, juggled Malay, Chinese, and Indian spices. In wet and lush Vancouver, my favourite foods were Hainan Chicken Rice, curry puffs, and dim sum with mustard. Years later, I fell in love with a man with a weakness for the Food Network and an extraordinary prowess in the kitchen.

2. Middle years

Recently, I have been asking friends and acquaintances about this tasteful organ: the tongue. They react as if I have asked them about their finances, or, worse, their genitalia. The tongue! We are put off by its sliminess, its redness, or maybe its odour. Our distaste for the tongue is ancient. When approached by predators—or, more commonly, cornered in a bus or on a stairwell, jostled in a crowd—people will often show their tongues: a slow, tense extension between the teeth. They have no idea they are doing this.

It is a warning sign that we *Homo sapiens* give, and respond to, subconsciously.

The tongue, when called up for duty, is as provocative as any organ.

(I apologize now to all the strangers I have crowded in order to test this theory. I speak the truth: I have witnessed many tongues.)

The difference between a kiss and a *kiss* is the tongue. Inside one's own mouth, there is precious little space for the intruder. Yet in it comes, tenderly or with bravado. In it comes, with both abandon and intent. The tongue, otherwise forgotten, knows how to give pleasure. It is more flexible than a finger; it can taste and swallow. It can lick, luxuriate, suck, wet, and then, as if that were not enough, tease with words. It is minutely sensitive to the feel of things and to their rising temperatures. The tongue asks for very little in return.

The great lovers of the world are well practised in the uses of the tongue.

When romance has faded, we sully the mouth. Kiss my ass, we scream. You suck. Lick me. Eat shit. We spit out our indignation. Could it be that we know, instinctively, that the tongue is the seat of the soul? The betrayer deserves a gob of our spit. We invite the heartbreakers to sweep their tongues through the gutter: only then will our vengeful desires be satisfied. Once enunciated, we tell ourselves, these words might liberate us from our pain.

The tongue is the Swiss Army knife of the human body, full of purpose, ever dangerous. The yodellers and the ululators know this. Their voices, abetted by the quickened curling and flicking of the tongue, call to the gods, the community, and the human soul. These reverberations are songs of joy, but in other times, in war and devastation, they are the ringing of despair. An ululation carries the mother's rage and the widow's tears. Our sisters, who have neither weapons nor drums, demand to be heard. We ignore these cries at our peril.

3. Dotage

After my mother died, I travelled alone to Hong Kong. I had a hope of finding the apartment where she had spent her childhood, of walking through the doors, of seeing what my mother had rarely spoken of. A friend of my mother's, a woman named Pinky, tried to assist me. I could understand her words, but my own Cantonese was broken and out of tune.

The spirit was willing, the heart beat fiercely, but the tongue was weak.

In silence, we walked through the crowded city. We stopped at a café, and I ordered my mother's favourite dish: *Dan dan mien*, Sichuan noodles so spicy they made my tongue burn and my eyes water. *Dan dan* refers to the wooden buckets used by vendors as they shout out their wares, and the phrase means "peddlar noodles." I ate in solidarity with my mother, so that my tongue would savour the same spices, so that I would find solace in the same act, the same taste.

Pinky wiped her eyes, paid the bill, and held my hand.

In old age, the teeth fall away but the tongue remains. The taste buds begin to degenerate, and the food we lusted after in our youth no longer brings the same pleasure. Dry-throated, we gravitate toward biscuits and toast. In all likelihood, when I'm old I will nourish myself with bowls and bowls of rice, slices of cucumber, and steamed green beans. But the tongue still remembers, doesn't it? Decades of swallowing and feeling, of preparing our children's food, of the bitterness and goodness of life. As the mind wanders back to our favourite dishes, how vividly those flavours return to us and make the taste buds prickle. Have we finally come to enlightenment, have we learned to glimpse the thing itself, the thing in its essence, without need of the material world? Here it comes now, a fleeting sensation, a taste, a lasting knowledge.

The final word, the last breath: we return to the tongue, just as we began. We are parched, it is hard to swallow. The tongue sends its signals to the mind: we are withering. We can no longer take in the world.

"Does nobody understand?" asked James Joyce not long before he died.

Soon, we will no longer have the capacity to make ourselves understood. Once more, our fingers reach out ineffectually, our vision blurs. All the thoughts in our minds, the beliefs we have carried, are destined to die with us.

What shall I have? A sip of wine? A kiss? Let it be a kiss. Let me feel my lover's fingertips once more against me, let me taste this sweetness one last time.

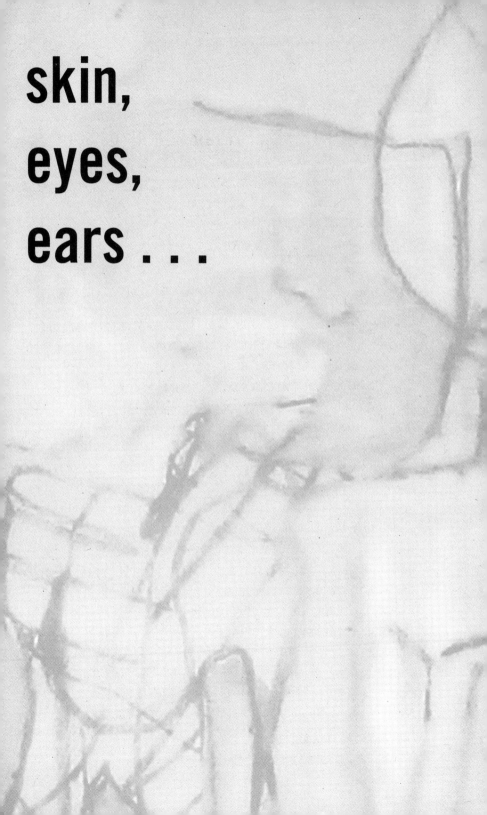

skin,
eyes,
ears . . .

What I Think of When I Think of Skin

Taiaiake Alfred

When I stand before thee at the day's end, thou shalt see my
scars and know that I had my wounds and also my healing.
—Rabindranath Tagore, *Stray Birds*

What is skin? Anatomically, our skin is an organ comprising twenty
square feet made up of three layers of constantly renewing cells
that serve as the waterproof container of our physicality. But I'd be
surprised if anyone thought that way about skin when they heard
the word. Skin . . . Who can forget being touched? The skin ignites
our passions, communicates our desires. Babies who are raised
without skin touch—stroking, cuddling, and kissing—suffer for the
neglect, making it nearly impossible for the adults they eventually
become to have meaningful and caring attachments. That's how
crucial a role our skin plays in the creation of love and affection
and human bonds. It is protection for our other organs, and it's also
the projection of our identities and emotions to others. The skin is
both intimate and public. It is a thin membrane linking our inside
life with our wider existence, and it's the pathway for our sensual
experience of the world and our relationships with other people.

If I close my eyes and think "skin," the first thing that comes to
mind is the feel of sun on my arms and back. With that thought
comes a flood of memories of sunburned days as a young US
Marine in tropical climes, when I just couldn't get enough of the
smell of the sultry air and salty ocean mist, the feel of the hot sun
on my face and my back. If I stay with the thought, I'm taken back

to the fading light of a Carolina summer's day: I'm in the middle of a boisterous crowd of laughing teenaged girls and shirtless Marines. A girl reclines languidly in the sand, the late-afternoon wind blowing soft curls across her face, which is set in a distant look that makes her seem uninterested in any of the boys or the games we are playing. I am fascinated by, of all things, the sun-speckled skin of her cheeks, shoulders, and breasts. I manoeuvre to sit next to her, but once in position I just sit there, not saying a word, trying to think of the perfect phrase that will make her want to stay with me and not go off with someone else when the sun goes down. I am taken by surprise when she looks over at me, smiles sweetly, and reaches out to gently touch my shoulder. She studies my own skin as she slowly draws her finger all the way down my arm, lingering for a minute when her fingertip connects with mine. She looks up at me with her green eyes, then drops her gaze and finger into the sand. With an arch of her eyebrows, she writes her phone number in the sand, then throws her head back and laughs as she quickly sweeps away the words and the numbers she's written.

Skin is the conduit of pleasurable sensations, but we all know it's usually the point of first contact and one of the main receptors of pain as well. Thinking back to my youth, I also remember when the spell of that summer day was broken and I was reminded that not all obsessions with skin are so romantic.

A few weeks after I'd met that girl, I was invited to go meet her parents. When I showed up at their house and knocked on the front door, her mother opened it slowly and peered around to look at me standing there on her front porch. When she saw me, the hard stare she was wearing gave way to a look of shock. "Oh my, thank God you're not a nigger!" she blurted.

I didn't know what to say.

"When my daughter told us she'd met someone and he wasn't white, we naturally assumed . . ."

"No, ma'am, I am not black," I said cautiously.

"But you are dark, though. What are you?" she asked.

"I'm Mohawk," I replied. "A Native."

"You mean you're an Indian? Really?" After thinking about what I'd said for a couple of seconds, a smile came across her face. She took me by the arm and said, "Come on in, son."

A dreamy setting for memories of one's youth it surely is, but the American South in the twentieth century was definitely not a time and place to escape from the implications of one's melanin or suntan. I often wondered if there was any escape. Had there ever been a society that was blind to skin colour? There had to have been times in history when the colour of one's skin didn't mean much to people. Hadn't I read that the ancient Greeks didn't bother themselves too much over skin tone? But that's probably only because they made slaves of *everyone* they conquered, whether they were light-, medium- or dark-skinned. That's not exactly an enlightened perspective.

People seem to think that modern-day Canada is a post-racist society. But I don't believe it; that's not my experience. Maybe, like the ancient Greeks, the people who are dominant now in this land, white people, no longer have to organize their ideas and institutions around skin colour to maintain themselves in the privileged position they have inherited from their brutishly racist ancestors. After all, the original landlords of this continent are (thought to be) conquered; we've been relentlessly de-cultured, and our freedom to be ourselves has been deposited alongside all the masks, canoes, and ladles in the museum. We are no longer a threat, and to most people it must seem like we crave nothing more than mercy and to be finally allowed to conform. To the now-dominant newcomers to our lands, the primitive racism of their forebears, which was so obsessed with assigning a person's worth on the basis of gradations of skin colour, must seem so obnoxious; it is certainly obsolete.

The ideas and attitudes of the past have served their purpose but are no longer needed to keep us in our place now that any idea we original landlords had about evicting the overbearing tenants and securing our homeland is out of the question. Now that the return of even a portion of our homeland or reparations for what we've lost is regarded as a laughable suggestion, the white descendants of the newcomers are able to tolerate us original people and to see us as humans, to admire our resiliency, to laud our insights. Many even admire brown skin and want to feel the non-white aesthetic by touching that which not so long ago was the mark of a scary and despicable savage.

When I was a boy, growing up on an Indian reserve outside of Montreal, notions of savagism and civilization were still present and acknowledged as facts in this country; it was a time and place where the colour of your skin determined the quality of your existence. In the new multicultural Canada, a lot of people don't realize that, until very recently, if you were Native, the identification card you were issued by the government reported not only such usual information as name and date of birth, but also the complexion of your skin: light, medium, or dark. I've never delved into the historical reasons for this, but I'm fairly certain it has something to do with the government's notion that it was worth taking note of the lighter skinned mixed-race, and presumably assimilated, members of the band and to distinguish them from the ones who were medium in tone—marked as potentially civilizable—and especially from the tawny ones, who were thought to be still mired in dark savagism, generations away from being able to appreciate the glories of mayonnaise and smooth jazz.

The ideas behind this imagined caste system were utter nonsense, of course, and a total failure, it turns out. I grew up with some fierce savages who were whiter in skin tone than the Minister of Indian Affairs himself. Although my own status card flagged me as dark-complexioned, I've always been disappointed by my instinct for good behaviour. I ended up disease-free and graduated from high school. I went to college instead of jail. I still have all of my teeth and can even speak English without an accent when I want to. So much for the tawny curse of the uncivilized.

The racial attitudes behind the government's fantasy caste system have always held sway in most people's minds in this country, yet when you think about it, they really make no sense at all, socially or scientifically. Take the example of me and my sister: I've always been "dark" to the Department of Indian Affairs, but really just medium brown compared with most people in the world; my sister, who shares my parentage, which includes our English grandmother, is as fair and sun-burnable as a human being could be. Growing up in such an intensely governed place as an Indian reserve and in such a thoroughly racially mixed situation as the Mohawk Nation, we were, of course, hyper-aware of how our skins affected our lives and others' perception of us.

My favourite nickname for my sister was French Fry. Being a bratty brother, I would get a real kick out of holding up a fry next to my sister's face and saying, "Look, twins. They're both so skinny and white." Ha ha. But I was just teasing in the way kids do, and I never thought of my sister as any less of a Mohawk than myself. Though by that time it was the late 1970s, and in those revolutionary days being a light-skinned Native had lost its lustre, so to speak. It had gone from being a privilege to being a cultural liability. So maybe I was being a bit cruel after all. It's no wonder she keeps reminding me of that story, even thirty years later. Anyway, I had put up with my share of racialized nicknames from the reserve's fairer set. I remember that all of the darker kids on our reserve were called *Rahonsti*, which means Black, or else something silly, like Chic-chocolate, all the time.

Still, the government failed in its bid to divide us on the lines of skin colour—and a good thing too, because they had plenty of other divide-and-conquer strategies that did work. You know why I can confidently say that they failed? Because my sister, la French Fry herself, ended up living, working, and raising her kids in our Mohawk community. It was me, the brown-skinned, brown-haired, brown-eyed one, who left the reserve as soon as I was able to and made a life outside of our small community. Our skin colours turned out to be imperfect predictors of our future in this country, and very unreliable indicators of what kind of Mohawks we were, civilized or not.

Skin colour is something we human beings naturally notice. But I learned early on in my life that it can never tell you anything meaningful about a person. Anyone reading these words who saw me on the street in Victoria would probably look at me and figure that I'm a Native, or at least the descendant of one, but that's as much as they'll know about me. And that's pretty useless information.

When I was a little boy, one of my chores was to help my father take his workboots off when he came home from his job. I looked forward to it. It was a son's act of devotion, sure, but also one of necessity. My father was an ironworker, and by the time he walked through the front door of our house late on a Friday night, he'd worked forty hours or more that week in the outdoors, thirty storeys up in the sky over New York City. Then he'd got in a car with a few other guys and driven the length of New York State, through the Adirondack Mountains, from the city to our reserve. On the way, he'd have drunk at least a six-pack of Schaefer beers. So he needed somebody to take off his boots.

If it was summertime, he'd have been working out in the sun without a shirt on, so I'd turn to my next job—which, now that I think of it, is probably responsible for my fascination with skin! He'd strip off his white T-shirt, and I'd climb up on the backrest of the couch, straddle his back, and start peeling skin off his shoulders and back. Every Friday night in the summer, I'd be peeling his back, the sunburned skin coming off in little strips and in big, saucer-sized patches. When he walked through the door of our house, he was a tough man with very dark skin, but after I was done my chore his back and shoulders would be a patchwork of pink and red and brown. He would sit on the couch and tell me to peel his back for him every time he came home, even though he'd flinch again and again as I peeled the skin to the flesh. This is what I would remember about him as he once again left on that journey across the great forest into the big city for another week of brutal work and hard sun thirty storeys up in the sky.

Scars are inscriptions, the work of others and ourselves, projected at the world. Fibroblast cells in our skin make collagen that we use to create the scar tissue that covers up the cuts and tears that have breached its multilayered integrity. In turn, we generate reasons, excuses, and fantasies that coalesce into flesh as scars and become stories we present and defend in the world and before the mirror.

I was badly scarred when I was younger. When I was in Marine Corps boot camp, the rifle I was firing blew up when I pulled the trigger, sending gunpowder, shattered brass, and pieces of gun metal flying up into my face. I picked tiny pieces of brass out of my face for a few months after that and lived with the redness of the powder burns around my mouth and chin for a while longer. You can't see any powder burns or little puncture wounds on my face anymore; the skin has since healed. But I swear I can still feel them. I have to suppress a slight flinch each time I put a rifle up to my chin and squeeze the trigger.

Could we as humans have evolved the ability to scar as a form of story, as a reminder to ourselves and others not to do dangerous or dumb things? Well, we are intelligent creatures, even ironworkers and Marines. Tattoos are a form of scarring, and they tell a story about a person too. Unlike other scars though, tattoos, especially these days, are more fashion statement than healed-over wound—there's not much risk or pain involved in acquiring these kinds of scars. They are constructed evidences of what we want people to think about us.

I have a couple of tattoos myself. The one on my right bicep is a screaming eagle with my Mohawk name spelled out below it. On my other arm, there is an Asian dragon with the letters USMC inscribed underneath. What do these tattoos tell you about me? I could say that they are marks of pride I chose to put on my body to forever proclaim my dual warrior heritage as a Native and as one of the few and the proud, Uncle Sam's Misguided Children. But that is such a self-conscious telling of my story. Actually, I got the screaming eagle tattoo on a dare. My buddy Jake and I were on a three-day drinking binge, and he said he'd pay for it if I had the guts to get tattooed by the old biker in the dingy parlour we'd wandered into. I got the other one a couple of months later because I couldn't stand the asymmetry of having one arm tattooed and the other blank.

Accidental and instrumental scars are the same in one way, though. The lessons they represent always take a while to sink in; stories take time to develop, and the physical scarring process takes a while to heal the wound. A human being sheds a layer of skin every day; over the course of a month, we take on an entirely new skin. But it takes two years of collagen and blood vessels working together to make even superficial scars fade to where no one notices them—though every scar will always bear some faint visible witness to what has happened. Scars never do completely heal over, and they remain with us as remnants and reminders of the deepest cuts and most severe wounds we've suffered.

I had a dream about my skin being scarred by a bear. In this dream, I stand rooted in place as trees, clouds, earth, and wind spin around me. A grizzly bear appears—I don't know how I know she is a female—and enters the maelstrom, circling me many times, with her eyes locked on mine. The effect is a terrifying, paralyzing ferocity. Suddenly everything falls still. The bear is frozen in place in front of me. It's like I am alive in the middle of a diorama. She stares right at or through me. In an instant, she presses her face against mine. She holds me in an intimate embrace and her claws dig hard into the skin of my forearms. In an unspoken language of the spirit through her liquid black eyes, she says, "I am going to hurt you, but I will not kill you." Her stare intensifies, and she breaks the skin as she drags her claws all the way down, leaving thick lines of scars on my arms. As soon as the embrace ends, the wounds heal over and I am left standing alone, without fear or pain, feeling clean and strong.

Eyes
Trevor Cole

I used to imagine being able to give my eyes back. There'd be a store somewhere, I figured, white-walled and bright, where I could take my eyes and trade them in for new ones. "Here," I'd say. "I don't want these anymore. I need a new pair."

"What's wrong with them?" the clerk would say. He'd pick up one of the eyes, I imagined, and examine it suspiciously.

"They're crap," I'd say. "They don't work right. Haven't as long as I can remember."

"Maybe we can fix them."

"Don't even bother. These eyes, they're nothing but trouble."

"New eyes are expensive," the clerk would say.

"They don't have to be great, just okay. I'm not going to be a big league baseball player or anything. Just give me some okay eyes. Be better than these stupid things."

I am roughly a half-century old, and my eyes have been a cause of heartache and frustration for me since about the age of two. It's hard to pinpoint the exact date, but whenever the moment came that I was asked, for the first time, to stand still in the backyard, look into the camera and smile, that's the day I first became annoyed with my eyes. Back then, possibly because there were no such things as cameras with built-in flashes, it was common practice for a backyard photographer to position herself with the sun over her shoulder, so that the light would fall smack on the front of her subject. A face full of sun, that's what you wanted in a family snapshot. "Honey, look up," I would hear. "Look up. And *smile!*" It was hard for me to smile, looking up, because my face was always bunched into a grimace. I might have been a mole the way my eyes burned in the bright sunlight. "Honey," I would hear. "Put your hand down. Take your hand away from your eyes!" Eventually whoever was taking the photograph, usually my mother, would give up and press the button. And so I have a collection of frozen images of my young self, alone and in groups, with my eyes mashed into slits or holding a small hand in front of my face, like a tiny Garbo, to ward off the searing rays.

My eyes were susceptible to more than just sunlight. That became all too clear during the summer of 1968, when I was eight years old. From June to September that year we lived on a farm on Prince Edward Island. My father was a starring actor in the Charlottetown Festival, and he preferred to live with his family outside the town, so the management of the festival found us an empty house on a working farm. As a boy, I liked nothing better than to spend my summer days romping around the fields, helping to feed the cattle in the barn, sitting on the wide, wooden wagon as the farmers baled up the hay. It was all very idyllic.

One day during the harvest I sat at the back of the wagon, at the top of a huge pile of hay bales, and felt my eyes getting itchy. Itchier than they'd ever been. Rubbing them seemed to help, but after a while the itching began to burn, and the only thing to do was rub harder. For hours, as the wagon filled up with hay, and the afternoon sun gradually sank toward the island's rolling hills, my fists burrowed away in my eyes.

When the tractor finally rolled into the barn and I climbed down from the wagon, I believe I said to one of the workers, "My eyes feel funny."

He said something to me along the lines of, "Son, you should get home."

I ran from the barn, across the property and into our house, calling for my mother. But my mother was out shopping, and my father was already at the theatre. So I was alone in the house when I pulled a chair over to the hallway mirror and stood up on it to see why my eyes felt so very strange.

What I saw horrified me. I had the eyes of a monster. The whites were a sickly yellow and bulging out grotesquely, surrounding the irises like rising bread dough. "I'm going blind!" I cried. And I ran outside, back toward the barn where I knew I would find someone. "I'm going blind!" I screamed.

I wasn't going blind, but it turned out I was terribly allergic to hay.

The next year, in Grade 4, a less dramatic but more life-altering problem surfaced. Sitting at the back of the portable classroom in Grand Valley, Ontario, I would watch the young teacher, Mr. Hobson, scrawling words and numbers on the chalkboard. Mr. Hobson had red hair, and his hands were long, thin, and freckled. I could see him well enough, but what he wrote on the board became increasingly fuzzy. I'd been a good student, but now I was having to ask the kids around me what it said up there. And if Mr. Hobson called on me to answer some question he'd written out, I had to resort to guessing. I don't recall that it ever occurred to me, at the age of nine, to admit that I couldn't see very well.

Mr. Hobson must have said something to my parents because before long I was sitting in an optometrist's chair, with a white-coated man before me holding little steel-rimmed monocles in front of my eyes while I read from a pyramid of letters on the wall, with its enormous capital *E* sitting at the top like a pharaoh of letters. A week or two later, I was fitted with my first set of glasses, with pale brown, horn-rimmed frames. The drive home from the optometrist's that day stands out as one of the most magical in my life because as I stared out the window, I saw for the first time that the trees rushing by along the side of the road weren't just big blobs of green. The world was suddenly a place of exquisite detail. "I can see all the leaves!" I exclaimed. And I know that beside me, my mother felt the pride of having done a great thing.

She didn't realize that she had also, unavoidably, sentenced me to a new kind of misery. Grand Valley, the little farming community to which we had moved from Toronto because my father was apparently hooked on rural living, had a population of eight hundred. The students of its single school tolerated a fairly narrow range of idiosyncrasy. Being the son of an actor, in a village of farmers, was already an enormous black mark against me. Now I was the only child in Grade 4 who wore glasses, which had a further toxic effect on my prospects. One can be called names and beaten up because he wears glasses only so many times before one begins to resent the glasses, and the eyes that require them, with a deep passion. It didn't help that my mother continued to buy, despite my objections, the most desperately un-cool horn-rimmed frames for me. Which explains why, when I reached the stage of wanting to impress girls and I had enough money of my own, I got rid of the glasses in favour of contact lenses.

Mind you, this was the 1970s version of contact lenses, which were not, it's fair to say, built for comfort to the same degree that lenses are today. There's a line in an otherwise inscrutable Kate Bush lyric that refers to "a plank in me eye"—and that's pretty much how these lenses felt. That was particularly true when a gust of wind would throw up grit from the sidewalk to work its way under the lenses and scrape against my corneas, or when the wind would simply dry out one of the lenses enough to make it adhere to the soft membrane like an old price sticker. It's true that women endure a great deal of pain for the sake of fashion, but they don't have anything on what I was willing to endure in order to be a guy who didn't wear glasses. And when soft lenses became strong enough to correct my truly appalling myopia, I was among the first in line.

One thing about those early soft lenses though: as relatively comfortable as they were, they weren't disposable. They had to be cleaned diligently lest bacteria invade the material and infect the eye. If you were a young man living away from home, cleaning your lenses properly wasn't always the priority it should have been. Or maybe you just had really crappy, infection-prone eyes, and no amount of meticulous lens cleaning could have saved you from the inevitable. Whatever the reason, before long I became intimately acquainted with the term *chalazion.*

A chalazion isn't an eyeball problem, it's an eyelid problem—an eyelid problem related, in my case, to ridiculously myopic eyeballs, which prompted me to stick bacteria-riddled lenses under lids that became infected and formed cysts that looked, when I blinked, as if I had stuffed a dried pea under each lid. The whole point of wearing contact lenses was to appear as attractive as possible, and I'm here to tell you that eyelid cysts aren't attractive at all.

Only ophthalmologists are allowed to deal with chalazions. Why? Because they require surgery. A doctor has to cut into the eyelids to remove them. It's not a hospital procedure, usually, but you do have to sit there in the examining room, gripping the arms of your chair while the ophthalmologist sticks a needle into your eyelid to freeze it. That's necessary because eyelids are terribly, terribly sensitive to pain—the pain of, say, a needle being shoved into them. Then you have to remain as still as possible while the doctor puts a clamp on your eyelid, twists it over to reveal the pink underside, and slices into the heart of the lid to dig out the cyst. After this, a bulky bandage is taped down hard over the eye to compress it and stop the bleeding. This bandage has to be worn for more than a week, and it is not appealing in the slightest.

When you have crappy eyes and ridiculous eyelids but refuse to wear glasses, you get chalazions repeatedly, no matter how vigorously and desperately you scrub your contact lenses. This means you have to return again and again to have needles and scalpels inflicted upon your eyelids. Eventually, this leads to more scar tissue than you really want to have in an eyelid, which leads to a thick, droopy lid rendered permanently unattractive, which also doesn't heal as quickly as it should after surgery.

You don't know this, of course, when you're a young man just trying to get ahead and not wear glasses. You don't know that a lid full of scar tissue doesn't knit together easily after it's been sliced into for the fifth or sixth time. Possibly the ophthalmologist doesn't know it either, because who on Earth is masochistic enough to submit himself to so many chalazion surgeries? It's uncharted territory.

This would help to explain what happened over a period of a few days in my mid-twenties. Once again, after the prescribed period, I'd removed my bandage and gone out into the city—I was living in Ottawa at the time—to attend to some errands. I was in a grocery store, as I remember, reaching for some item on a shelf, when suddenly a curtain of blood descended over the surface of my eye. The incision under the lid had let go and was now bleeding profusely as I stood in the middle of the store. I had to ask a checkout clerk for a Kleenex, which I jammed against my eye until eventually the bleeding stopped.

Ophthalmologists are hard people to pin down, even for an emergency appointment. So every once in a while over the next few days—while I was at work, on a date, driving—the blood curtain would fall. I learned to keep a package of Kleenex handy.

The last quarter-century hasn't been nearly as dramatic for me, eye-wise. Antihistamines have taken care of the allergies. I wear sunglasses when it's even a little bit sunny. I've endured the same slow deterioration of my reading vision as have most people my age, and for a good many of those years I gave up on contacts and accepted the fact that I was a guy who wore glasses. Laser eye surgery seemed an option, but no, I'm too myopic. And the fact is, laser surgery could have taken away the one thing my eyes do well. There has always been, no matter what, a zone of clarity in front of my face. Once it extended about a foot from my eyes, far enough that I could lie in bed with a book or a comic propped on my chest and read it without glasses. That zone has shrunk over the years, it's now down to about three or four inches, but it's still there. When I take off my glasses and hold something—a picture, a ladybug, the palm of my hand—a few inches away from my face, I see it as sharp and clear as I could hope for. The rest of the world is a watery haze, but three or four inches away, that's the sweet zone. And when I want to see myself clearly, the way a man sometimes needs to do as he ages, such a narrow region of clarity allows me, or forces me, to lean in to the mirror. It insists that I look into my own eyes with an intimacy that, more often than not, I find comforting. If my eyes haven't given me much over the years, at least they've always given me that. These days, even if I could trade my eyeballs for a new set, I'm not sure I would. Not without a guarantee that I could keep that sweet zone.

The Covert Ear

Margaret Thompson

On a Saturday morning in late July 1959, my ears struck a blow for personal freedom.

My school in Wimbledon had a strict dress code. For eight years I had, with my contemporaries, toed the line: navy skirt; long-sleeved blouses in light blue or a yellow that could be anywhere between King Alfred daffodil or dying primrose, depending on the garment's age; navy cardigan or sweater; navy blazer or overcoat; and in summer, hideously limp blue or yellow rayon dresses whose seams shone after ironing. These were just the basic requirements. Like any Draconian laws, they were accompanied by a host of regulations that covered the fine details and adroitly blocked every personal inclination: hair beyond shoulder length to be tied back; berets or the summer option, the charmless panama, to be worn at all times in the street; shoes to be above all flatly sensible, and either black or brown; white gloves in summer; divided skirts, worn for field games, to be no shorter than four inches above the knee—this last to be checked in the event of dispute by the wearer kneeling while a tape measure was deployed. It is probably unnecessary to add that makeup was forbidden. And all jewellery, except for modest wrist watches, came under the same ban. En masse, we were impressively . . . uniform.

For the most part, these rules sparked no rebellion, though seniors might occasionally chafe at the impossibility of making any significant fashion statement. It was the 1950s, after all, and there is quite a lot to be said in favour of school uniforms. But to reach the age of eighteen with only weekends and holidays as outlets for personal expression is to experience a degree of repression that threatens to become stifling. The morning after I passed through the school gates for the last time, I had my ears pierced.

A pretty freakish move for the time, when pierced ears were regarded as the preserve of gypsies and other foreigners, all dubious. Not many establishments offered the service; finding a small jeweller with a card in the corner of the window—Ears Pierced—and being ushered to a dusty backroom that doubled as a storeroom felt almost illicit, like seeking out an abortionist, but without the desperation. I'd heard stories about DIY versions of this procedure with threaded needles and corks, and quailed briefly. I was reassured when the assistant lined up alcohol and gauze and rendered my earlobes numb with some kind of local anesthetic after marking the puncture sites and satisfying herself they were level.

"Hold still now," she urged. "It won't hurt."

She was right. But the noise was a shock. I never did see what she used, but it bit through my ears with a dreadful crunch, as if giant teeth were forcing their way through stiff yet rubbery plastic.

Home I went, proudly wearing sleepers, which I was supposed to turn every day. Infection made this ritual unpleasant, but I gritted my teeth—il faut souffrir pour être belle, or libre, come to that—and persevered.

I have worn earrings ever since.

So I exchanged membership in one conformist herd for another and joined the ranks of those humans in every age and culture who have enlisted their ears as props for an astonishing variety of embellishment.

The human form of the ears we share as basic equipment with all other vertebrates is peculiarly suitable for self-adornment. Ears come in pairs, attached symmetrically to the sides of the head. They are stationary, since only a talented few can waggle them, unlike, say, rabbits, which can swivel theirs in any direction, independently, stand them up and lay them down at will. Above all, these gristly appendages with their little fleshy lobes don't seem to *do* anything because their work, corralling the unviewable and protecting the invisible, is essentially covert. So they suffer the usual fate of those perceived to be at a loose end—a job is found for them.

Every part of them has been stabbed, punctured, pierced, and studded; ornaments punctuate, dangle, skewer, and clasp; lobes have been stretched to the shoulders by weights and inserts. It is even possible to find precise instructions on the Internet, complete with photographs, for excising neat wedges of the curved outer edge of the helix in order to have pointed Pixie ears. After cutting a triangular chunk out of your upper ear, they suggest, "Sterilize a needle with a lighter, thread with fishing line or yarn, and sew your ear back together in the desired shape." And then, "Put some tape round your ear to hold it together and prevent strain on the stitches." An earlier instruction on the list—"Score some rubbing alcohol. Take a few shots"—betrays the intent, but the photographs come from a cosmetic surgeon's website. If your inclination is to roam the world as a Spock clone, you can.

But lingering over appearance in this way, fascinating though it may be, is a typically human preoccupation with the trivial. What marvels it ignores!

Consider that outer ear for a minute, unembellished. Among our fellow vertebrates it comes in a dizzying array of shapes and sizes, from the flamboyant excess of African elephants and certain species of bat to the minimalist openings, hidden beneath special tiny feathers, in most birds. Each one functions as a conduit, a built-in satellite dish to collect and focus sound waves, but their infinite variety of form is also a hymn to the power of natural selection and adaptation. Those enormous waving ears help elephants not only to hear—and to hear over several miles in a subsonic range undetectable by humans, incidentally—but also to regulate body temperature, essential in a creature so large. Because a bat hunts by echolocation in the dark, its very survival depends on the acuity of its ears; so does the barn owl's, whose asymmetrical ears—the left, lower and pointing upwards; the right, higher and pointing down—permit an exceptionally accurate triangulation of the source of sound, together with the ability to hear the heartbeat of a mouse hidden under three feet of snow. And anyone who has heard the walloping that wind produces in an unprotected microphone will realize why that baffle of tiny feathers over a songbird's ear has evolved.

In the face of such evolutionary masterpieces, our own ears seem a little tame. True, some appreciate their erotic possibilities for nibbling, nuzzling, and filling with sweet nothings, a fortuitous result of the command centres for sexual arousal and hearing being next-door neighbours in the brain. They are certainly the most sculptural of all our visible parts, delicate constructions of curves and whorls, ridges and folds and indentations—shell-like, for sure, but a little disappointing as a result, a little derivative, not quite up to the standards of original design that a superior creature such as ourselves might reasonably expect. There is more to the ear, though, than meets the eye.

It starts with those very complexities of the outer ear. Each one is unique, as individual and identifiable as a fingerprint. At the same time, each one preserves dim echoes of the distant past of our species, reminders of our long evolutionary journey. At the sixth month of gestation, the human ear closely resembles those of primates such as the Barbary ape: it is flatter on top and pointed. That similarity disappears, of course, but many humans have a very slight thickening of the helix about a third of the way down the outer curve of the ear. This is called Darwin's tubercle, and marks where the point of the ear once formed in our ancestors. There is something thrilling, and at the same time sobering, about that inconspicuous bump.

Most animals can use their ears to convey their feelings or intent, but humans are duds in that department. That doesn't mean our ears are uninformative. Just like the Hapsburg nose, ears can be a family affair. In 1937, a researcher studying cup-shaped ears traced the deformity, affecting twenty-two members of the same family, back through five generations on the maternal side to an orphan girl of German origin. Certain conditions, such as Down and Turner syndromes, include small, low-set ears as one of their characteristic features. A crease in the earlobe of a newborn suggests Beckwith-Wiedemann syndrome, a congenital growth disorder.

There are more secrets within. That shell-like outer ear has many practical functions, funnelling and intensifying sound waves, locating their source, and protecting the eardrum from injury; even the lobe does its bit, providing central heating through its lavish blood supply. But it is also a portal, an ornate entrance to one of the very few shortcuts to the brain itself, a hidden passageway full of marvels. The very names of the landmarks along the way through the ear are reminiscent of a fantastic Otherworld where magic rules and Orcs might lurk. I can almost see the plot outline: our hero, a tremulous, nameless orphan, sets out alone on a journey filled with impossible tasks and obstacles to find his true identity. He slips through the Navicular Fossa, ducks under the Tragus, and finds himself sliding helplessly, faster and faster, down a waxy slope. He hurtles with a resounding thud into the Tympanic Membrane, which gives beneath his weight, but he sees that he has set in motion the Ossicles—Malleus the Hammer, Incus the Anvil, and Stapes the Stirrup. He rides the Stirrup until it taps the Oval Window. But now he is in a different, watery world, adrift on the waves in the Cochlea. Desperately he searches for the only hair that will bend to his particular touch in the Organ of Corti to fire a signal to the brooding mainframe. And lo! Our hero is revealed at last as the plangent opening chord of the Elgar Cello Concerto—or the drip of a tap, if you savour irony.

Truth is, magic *does* rule here. The process by which small disturbances of the air are amplified and translated so that we hear them is little short of alchemy. Strictly speaking, the ear is a transducer, efficiently changing energy from one form into another, but that is a chilly definition for what goes on every time we listen to Beethoven's Ninth or the baby crying or the conversation behind us on the bus. The invisible is perceived; the unknowable is translated; the ephemeral is captured. All this, and balance too, for the ear is a multitasking organ, and those microscopic mineral particles brushing against the hairs in the semi-circular canals keep us on an even keel—or not, as anyone who, like me, has reeled off the Tilt-A-Whirl to vomit in the bushes can testify.

Despite all this, ears get little overt respect. They are retiring organs, completely unobtrusive until something goes wrong. Until that day, nobody spares them a thought. Yet they have worked their way, nonetheless, into our thinking and our language; obviously, they have significance. If someone has perfect pitch or a gift for mimicry, we say he or she has a good ear. To have someone's ear is to have access to the powerful and, by extension, to be influential oneself. A stinging rebuke, courtesy of Rabelais, is a flea in the ear. Unplanned action is playing by ear. When we are eagerly attentive, we are all ears. Linguistically, we are up to our ears in ears . . .

Shakespeare certainly found inspiration in their metaphorical possibilities. "Friends, Romans, countrymen," bawls Antony at a mob hostile to the very idea of listening to him, "lend me your ears!" When they do, grudgingly, he manipulates his audience into a howling lust for revenge and turns them loose against the conspirators. Thoroughly nasty Iago whispers his insinuations in Othello's ear and poisons a relationship for no good reason. And the most graphic example—both literal and figurative—of the damage caused by pouring poison into ears comes from the ghost of Hamlet's father lamenting his own untimely end at the hands of his brother, and the ensuing abuse of "the whole ear of Denmark" by the phony tale of a snake bite. Shakespeare's physiology may be a bit suspect but there is nothing shaky about his capacity for horror:

> Upon my secure hour thy uncle stole,
> With juice of cursed hebona in a vial,
> And in the porches of mine ear did pour

The leperous distilment; whose effect
Holds such an enmity with blood of man
That swift as quicksilver it courses through
The natural gates and alleys of the body,
And with a sudden vigour it doth posset
And curd, like eager droppings into milk,
The thin and wholesome blood; so did it mine,
And a most instant tetter bark'd about,
Most lazar-like, with vile and loathsome crust,
All my smooth body.

"In the porches of mine ear . . ."—that phrase has haunted me ever since I first read *Hamlet* as a teenager plagued, ironically, by various unlovely skin conditions. I am uneasily aware that the ear is a breach in the head's defences, an opening that cannot be closed, vulnerable to intruders. There is nothing unique about my queasiness; people have been frightening each other with stories about insects that take up residence in the ear and bore through the brain for centuries. While these may be the urban myths of their time, we retain their spirit still; after all, we still call one of those insects by the name our Anglo-Saxon forebears gave it more than one thousand years ago, even though earwigs probably wouldn't be caught dead in a human ear, and even if they were, certainly wouldn't get any farther unless they developed the ability to mine through the densest bone of the skull.

Reason may assert we have little to fear from alien incursions, but John Hanning Speke probably took little comfort from that notion, if he ever entertained it. He is the nineteenth-century explorer who accompanied Richard Burton on a celebrated and harrowing journey to find the source of the Nile and was actually the one who staggered on alone and half-blind, while Burton was ill, and found it in Lake Victoria. More to our point, he was sheltering in his tent during a storm one night and noted in his journal that the interior of the canvas "became covered with a host of small beetles, evidently attracted by the glimmer of the candle." He tried to brush them away, but exhaustion made him fall asleep without getting rid of them. Later he was woken by one of the beetles crawling into his ear and could not dislodge it. The beetle apparently became desperate to escape: "he began with exceeding vigour, like a rabbit in a hole, to dig violently away at my tympanum."

Speke had no mineral oil at hand, so he tried to flush the insect out with melted butter. When that had no effect, he tried to spear it with his knife and succeeded in killing it, mangling his ear further in the process, without being able to remove the corpse. Inevitably, infection followed; his face and neck swelled and he broke out in boils. Speke matter-of-factly describes the appalling result: "For many months the tumour made me almost deaf, and ate a hole between the ear and the nose, so that when I blew it, my ear whistled so audibly that those who heard it laughed. Six or seven months after this accident happened, bits of the beetle—a leg, a wing, or parts of the body—came away in the wax."

The incident speaks volumes about the toughness of nineteenth-century explorers in Darkest Africa, but it also takes the phrase "to put a bug in your ear" to a whole new level. I can still hear distant echoes of my best friend's mother, a Red Cross nurse, dispensing homespun wisdom: "Never put anything smaller than your elbow in your ear!"

Loathsome crusts and invading insects aside, the threat of that attack through the vulnerable ear still resonates. How often nowadays is our ear abused by the half-truths, self-justifications, demonizations, slanderous vilifications, and downright lies of those with power and authority of every kind? How often is debate just another term for name-calling and shouting down your opponent? How cynical have we become because we feel we cannot trust what anybody says anymore? The unfortunate earwig has something to say about all this too: from the late Middle Ages to the end of the eighteenth century, the noun also signified a whisperer, a flatterer, or a sycophantic follower, and used as a verb, *to earwig* meant to

pester with private importunities or to influence by secret communications. There's a good case to be made to resurrect such usages;
they would be useful nowadays, if only to enliven the headlines.
Imagine the possibilities: "Revolt in Harper Cabinet: I Am Not an
Earwig, Claims Ex-Minister."

These voices in our ears—this toxic disinformation, misinfor-
mation, prevarication, distortion—are all part of the general clamour.
Every day we face a barrage of noise and endure it because we are
so accustomed to the background roar. Admittedly, the ear has a
remarkable ability to filter sound; anyone who has allowed a companion's voice to fade into inaudibility while he or she eavesdrops on
someone else's conversation will have experienced it in action. But
everyone has a list of egregious rackets that are well nigh unbearable
and all too commonplace: chainsaws, leaf blowers, motorbikes with
defective exhausts, and rap are high on my personal list, and I suspect
that every kind of music ever invented would find its detractors
somewhere, clapping their hands over their ears and complaining
bitterly about the depraved tastes of others. Worst of all, though, we
are assailed by a welter of noise that means nothing, that solves no
problems, lightens no darkness, and sparks no inspiration—a roiling
tide of trivialities and ephemeral junk screaming for our attention as
if every last scrap of it were vitally important.

"Heard melodies are sweet," said Keats, "but those unheard/Are
sweeter."

Ah. Silence.

In our modern Babel, we put a premium on silence
mainly because it is so very hard to find. Silence, we say, is golden.
While the young shut out the world by plugging themselves into
iPods and filling their heads with noise, weary adults yearn for peace
and quiet, seek out places far from "civilization" for their weekends
and vacations, and sigh with contentment when they achieve tranquil
days and undisturbed nights. "It was so *quiet*," they enthuse when they
return to the traffic and sirens and hustling crowds of ordinary life.

The therapeutic and spiritual value of silence has long been recognized. Ancient Eastern religions approach enlightenment through meditation, stripping away all non-essentials, emptying the mind of distractions so that it may finally be receptive to illumination. Many religious orders—the Trappists, for example—lived in silence, the better to contemplate the divine.

On a far more mundane level, our own behaviour sometimes demonstrates the same principle. When we enter a church, we instinctively lower our voices, whisper, or sit in silence. We walk with a minimum of clatter, subduing our lumpen corporeal presence as much as possible, even if we are non-believers, in a kind of respect for the spiritual. You will see the same reaction in great libraries, or art galleries, in the presence of masterworks—anywhere, it seems, where people set aside the minutiae of their existence to focus intently on some manifestation of the life of the mind.

On a recent visit to Canterbury Cathedral, I found myself pausing at the foot of the steps leading to the high altar. Between the steps and the altar itself lay an expanse of empty stone floor, and halfway along it and slightly to one side, quite alone, stood a large candle. The flame burned unwaveringly in the stillness. No voice offered an explanation, but I knew why it was there. I, and everyone else who passed that way, lingered to acknowledge the only memorial to mark the exact place where Thomas à Beckett was murdered by Henry II's knights, standing rapt in a silence filled with the small reverberations of that ancient building, contemplating immensities: loyalty and betrayal, expediency, the sad withering of friendship, the horror and sacrilege muted now to a quiet grief in the long drift of time.

Ironically, we not only think more deeply and clearly in silence, but we also hear better. As distractions diminish, our perceptions become more and more acute. Anyone who has stood in a silent cave with all light extinguished will vouch for this. Slowly, the impenetrable darkness fills with tiny sounds that were inaudible before: secret drips, infinitesimal shifts, the muffled thud of one's own pulse, the whisper of respiration. Astronauts have the same experience; their observation of the absolute silence of space is accompanied by the tiny sounds of their bodies at work, even the movements of their mouths and eyes. Which rather begs the question: if silence is not actually silent, what is it?

For eccentric American composer John Cage, there was no such thing as silence. He reached this conclusion after experiencing sensory deprivation, during which he was still aware of both a high and a low tone that he was told were the sounds of his nervous system and heart. He believed implicitly that the function of music was "to sober and quiet the mind, thus rendering it susceptible to divine influences." He had long discarded harmony—claiming to have "no ear"!—and, influenced by the concept of the emptiness of all things in Zen Buddhism and the completely white or black canvases of Robert Rauschenberg, eventually abandoned all focus on structure to embrace chance or accidental sound. His most famous—or infamous—work, *4'33"*, is a logical destination in this musical journey.

At its first performance, in a concert hall near Woodstock, New York, in 1952, the pianist walked onto the stage, sat down, and played nothing for four minutes and thirty-three seconds, using a stopwatch to mark the beginning of each movement by closing the piano lid and the end by opening it. The back door of the hall was open, and during the performance trees rustled outside, rain pattered on the roof, and the baffled audience shuffled and muttered, got up and left, and finally burst out in indignant uproar. Clearly, the chance sounds *were* the music for Cage; those four minutes, thirty-three seconds of attention were simply the frame for the accidental sounds. Equally obviously, the piece would never be the same twice.

One answer to the question, then, may be that silence is all the sounds of life that are discernible only when we have deliberately stripped away the noise that obscures them.

For many, silence is undeniably a solace. Yet teeming urban life in industrialized society habituates people to constant noise, producing young who find silence threatening, not therapeutic, something to be filled with sound as quickly and deafeningly as possible. At the other end of the scale are those for whom silence is normality, the profoundly deaf who have never heard anything. Between the over-taxed ears of the one group and the silence of the other lies a gulf of incomprehension. Those who can hear place a high value on this sense; they cannot imagine having to do without it and consider its lack a terrible disadvantage and its decline a catastrophe. To them, deafness is a defect. In their minds, anything that might mitigate that impairment is obviously desirable; it is inconceivable that a deaf person would not clutch at any opportunity to hear. Cochlear implants, for example. How could anybody reject a device that might enable a child to hear sound and therefore learn to speak?

Yet many deaf people, especially those born deaf, regard such implants as intrusive, thoroughly wrong-headed, unconscionable violations of individual rights. They do not consider themselves defective. They have evolved their own culture and language, their own way of dealing with the world, with no help from their ears. Insisting that their lives would be so much better if they could hear is insultingly condescending. To them, hearing is simply unneces-sary and unwanted.

So Lamb's "indispensable side-intelligencers" aren't, necessarily. But I am glad I have mine, in reasonable working order—though I sense a gradual deterioration, a growing tendency to misinterpret or simply miss, that will probably culminate in my sporting one of those dingy pink-beige devices (a tone that flesh never assumed this side of the undertaker's) in my ear one day. As vertebrate ears go, mine are neither the top of the line nor the bottom; they are neat and amusingly shaped, but unlikely to be fondled lovingly by people crooning, "Butter ears!" as my basset hounds' frequently are. Never mind. I am grateful for my own ears' secret complexity, for their clever magic tricks that allow me all the sounds of the world, including its silence. Maybe if I listen hard enough to that, I will one day hear the gods whispering; if not, the listening will be enough.

brain,
hands,
feet . . .

The Human Brain

Lorna Crozier

1.

Over and over, it quotes Descartes, "I think; therefore I am," though it doesn't really know what it is. Like a mirror, it cannot see itself. It knows its shape and size only from images of other brains reproduced in books and films or on computer screens, though once, there was a picture of itself backlit on the wall in a doctor's office. These glimpses have led it to propose several metaphors: a walnut minus the shell, a cauliflower turning grey and soft, the bioluminescent cap of a Brazilian mushroom, recently discovered, that glows green in the forest at night. Here, the brain halts the thought and corrects itself: in the dark bowl of the skull, it glows blue.

2.

The brain believes in ghosts. It knows they exist because it creates them. Think of the missing arm or leg, its phantom pain strong enough to make a grown man bite into a piece of leather. Think of the crying of an unborn child tucked into one of its pleats. The brain hears it every night and sends the audio to the heart, which, though this is biologically impossible, aches.

3.

Lean and hungry, it thinks too much. It worries and plans and rehearses and resents and worries and conspires and regrets and divides and supposes and forgets. Then there's the dreaming. Every night it's driven to create a vast emporium inside the head, a mental Cirque du Soleil, a solar system yet unnamed, with all its suns and moons and people from the past, a bus driver met only once, a mother pushing a carriage full of cabbages, a boy thin and beautiful as a cheetah, a lonely child who is merely the sleeper growing old.

4.

Its right frontal lobe is the seat of *Homo sapiens*' sense of humour. Those with lesions there often exhibit silly, euphoric behaviour and inappropriate laughter. They love slapstick. Given the choice, they'd rather spend an evening with the Three Stooges than with Mary Walsh or George Carlin. To map humour's brainy home address, scientists have designed a test that presents the following joke with multiple punchlines: A teenager is being interviewed for a summer job. "You'll get fifty dollars a week to start off," says the boss. "Then after a month, you'll get a raise to seventy-five dollars a week."

Punchline selection:
1. "I'd like to take the job. When can I start?"
2. "That's great. I'll come back in a month."
3. "Hey, boss, your nose is too big for your face!"

You can guess which of the three alternatives right-frontal damaged patients are likely to choose. And which one those with uninjured brains pick as the right funny answer. But which group would choose number 1? Has their brain damage been undiagnosed? Are their wounds invisible? Can you imagine how boring such people would be as a husband or a wife, even as a friend you'd meet only once a week for lunch? Wouldn't you rather live with a cushion that farts, a brother who slaps the other brother behind you when you duck, a banana peel left in the middle of the floor every night in the hallway that leads from your bedroom to the bathroom door?

5.

Meanwhile, the body. The brain forgets it is only one part. It sits high in its throne and commands. Sometimes the legs will not move and the brain throws a fit. Makes the teeth bite through the tongue, the eyes roll back, the limbs thrash like those of a swimmer who's thrown himself into an arctic sea. The brain is a bully, a buffoonish brute that loves to alliterate. It is buffed from hefting all those weighty burdens, bruised, belligerent, baffled, barren—that's what it comes to—barren. It's not the mind with all its clout, but the rest of the body that creates, without cognition, the anoetic miracle of flesh and bones.

6.

The brain is its own mole, digging in the dirt of dreams. It is its own sea, drowning in dead fish and salt. Since it has never felt the wind, it takes the sky's word for it. As well: sunlight on the eyelids, the brushstroke of leaves across a shoulder, the spit of rain on the forehead. Its synapses hum like telephone wires thickened with hoarfrost. It takes the heart's word for sorrow, the foot's for lost, the thumb's for what-if. Most days the brain is a beggar proffering an empty cup that seeks the currency of the unimagined, something real and solid its speculations can't make disappear.

7.

The tongue is a piece of the left frontal lobe severed at some stage of evolution, fallen into the mouth, blundering, reluctant. Of limited mental capacity, the tongue would rather taste and talk than ponder. The brain absolves itself, denies, pretends to be no one's keeper. Disowns the tongue when it leaps from savoury to stupid for no good reason, when it scats the scatological just to shock. The tongue believes it is more than just a hunk of meat, though it's no different from a cow's or pig's. If the tongue were soaked in vinegar like theirs, the brain surmises, the toughness and the smart talk would be leached away.

8.

Hypothesis: The amygdala, the almond-shaped subcortical structure in the temporal lobe, decides which experiences are significant enough to store.

> Subject: twenty-six male rabbits.
> Research team: National Institute of Mental Health in Bethesda, MD.
> Experiment: The rabbits were presented with two different tones. One resulted in nothing. The other was followed in five seconds by a shock to the feet.

Rabbits with undamaged brains learned the consequences and avoided the shock by moving a wheel beneath them. Rabbits whose amygdala had been disabled failed to learn such a response to the shock-depicting tone. What happened to the latter group, over and over, is obvious. Yet if you were a kid in the 1960s, you will remember when a rabbit's foot meant good luck. It swung from rearview mirrors, it hung from key chains, and sometimes it was dyed blue or pink.

9.

The brain's oldest part, reptilian, basks on a ledge balanced on the top of the spinal cord. Though it likes to sleep, its eyes stay open and do not blink. It's as muscled as a lizard's tail—a quick flick and you flee from danger or throw a punch. It is here, too, that dreams are hatched, if you can call it that. Each one has a single tooth to chew through its egg's leather casing. Called an egg tooth, soon it disappears. Soft-mouthed and squamous, the dream then rises to the brain's higher chambers and belly-slides into your sleep.

10.

The brain thinking about itself is thinking about the brain thinking. The brain not thinking about itself is thinking about the brain not thinking. Many things don't have brains and they do just fine. Trees, amanita mushrooms, geraniums, spermatozoa, million-year-old stones. The brain thinking about million-year-old stones can't help but wonder what's on their minds.

11.

"O, full of scorpions is my mind, dear wife!"; out of mind, out of his mind, to be of one mind, reminded, "And Archimedes, the famous Mathematician, was so intent upon his Problems, that he never minded the Soldier who came to kill him" (Swift); frame of mind, on my mind, you put me in mind of, your mind's eye, "The lads you leave will mind you/Till Ludlow tower shall fall" (Housman); mind your manners, mind your tongue, if you don't mind, presence of mind, absent-minded, speak one's mind, "Never mind about your handwriting; but mind you write" (Disraeli); time out of mind, keep me in mind, mind your step, "I wish either my father or my mother . . . had minded what they were about when they begot me" (Sterne); mind over matter, in one's right mind, mind your own business, mind the stove, the stairs, the rafter—mind your head! I'll mind, I'll mind; "All the efforts of the human mind cannot exhaust the essence of a single fly" (Aquinas); never mind, dear friends, never mind, "Not at rest or ease of Mind, they sate them down to weep" (Milton).

12.

Strange, the things a brain can get used to: trepanning, electric shocks, lobotomies, bruising, lesions, hailstorms inside the skull. There's now a scan that can detect a trace of iron in the tissues, a sign that the brain once bled. Following a stroke, one of its lobes, until then an understudy, steps onto the stage and belts out the libretto because the lead soprano has fallen mute. The brain learns to use a metaphoric walker, a magnifying glass to read the writing on the wall. It drags a dead limb up and down its many stairways, learns to live with familiar pieces of itself turned suddenly remote and cold as ice floes. And like ice floes in the northern seas, they drift.

13.

Is it possible for the brain to live in parity with the heart? Can it feel? Here is a true story: a British neurosurgeon, who was also a poet, had to remove a tumour from a patient. As his knife sliced into the cerebral cortex, the man cried out, "Leave my soul alone! Leave my soul alone!" A chill entered the operating room. No one moved. The surgeon, still bent over the patient's head, held the scalpel in mid-air. Around the table, all of them, religious or not, stared at the brain naked in its bowl of bone. Stunned into silence by that cry, everyone waited in the harsh light, afraid the brain had more terrifying things to say.

Hand Over Hand

Kathy Page

A woman's hands are supposed to be slender, pale, long-fingered, soft, with even, oval nails: so say the palmists, and the admen too. Glance in any contemporary magazine and you'll see many female hands that look elegant, sensitive, and decorative, none that appear strong or capable. As Erving Goffman pointed out in his photo essay "The Feminine Touch," we rarely see commercial imagery in which a woman's hands grasp, manipulate, or hold.

A woman with the right kind of hands can make a fair living as a hand model, but that's not an option in my case because whatever they are *supposed* to be like, my hands are square-palmed, strong, and big-thumbed, with sturdy, well-knuckled fingers, generously padded at the tips—spatulate,[1] without a doubt. The thumbs bend right back (a sign, apparently, of either generosity, both emotional and financial, or of extravagance and recklessness).

My palm measures nine centimetres across, which, for a hand, is wide; stretched out, the span from little finger to thumb is twenty-two centimetres. There's a substantial muscular bulge between my index finger and thumb, and the overall impression is of breadth and capability: these are working hands. But what else do they say about me? There is this feeling or hope that somehow all of our existence—

---

[1] Sherlock Holmes is a great one for observing hands. Spatulate fingers occur in "The Adventure of the Solitary Cyclist," where Holmes struggles with the interpretation: "'You will excuse me, I am sure. It is my business,' said he, . . . 'I nearly fell into the error of supposing that you were typewriting. Of course, it is obvious that it is music. You observe the spatulate finger-ends, Watson, which is common to both professions?'"

both our character and our fate—is written in our hands, and at some point, most of us succumb: drunk at a party, or in a shadowy tent at the fairground, or in some run-down, off-beat apartment above a shop, in the shade of a *palapa* on a beach in Mexico, we offer our hands to a stranger's gaze: the lines and mounds, the scars and coloration—it's all supposed to signify. Every hand is different, the theory goes, and is both a record and a prediction of its owner's destiny. In his 1897 opus *The Study of Palmistry for Professional Purposes and Advanced Purposes*, Comte C. de Saint-Germain, writing of what he calls "the woman 'womanly', the mother, the sweetheart, the daughter; the woman of the home," remarks that

> First of all, that the Tips of these Fingers are neither Spatulate nor Square; they belong evidently to the Conical type, but not often so pronounced. The possessors of such fingers are ruled by impulse, rather than calculation; they are predisposed to love beautiful things; they pass quickly from the acme of felicity to the lowest depth of despair; they need excitement in their lives and are not—alas!—they are not always constant . . . In this hand there are no Knots. Especially the First joint is decidedly smooth, meaning, as you know, the absence of logical, philosophical bent of the mind.

I'm clearly not *the woman of the home*. So am I what he calls *the woman of genius*? I am supposed to be both practical and artistic. The robust build of my hands suggests that I might be a sculptor or a builder, a musician or a stenographer. I've worked as a carpenter and did once aspire to be an artist, but ended up as a writer. But clearly the other possibilities still suggest themselves, and at academic job interviews, I have more than once noticed a panellist surreptitiously studying my hands and sensed her imagining me to be an impostor—a mechanic or an escaped convict, trying to con my way into the ivory tower.

The rest of me is fairly small, so these big, strong hands can seem out of scale. When I was a girl, the contrast was greater still: my hands looked as if they might have been grafted on, as if you might lift my grubby schoolgirl sleeve and find a raised white scar and two rows of dots circling each wrist.[2]

My mother has small hands. She chews her nails and hates herself for doing it. Her hands feel the cold, and she likes, where possible, to wear gloves—cotton or lined leather according to the season. She has perhaps twenty pairs, stashed in coat pockets and in a basket in the closet, as well as a sub-collection of gardening gloves kept in the garage, but because of the size of my hands, I can't borrow any of them. Gloves or no gloves—and leaving aside writing—everything I do ingrains my hands with dirt, or adds fresh cuts or abrasions. Mum's hands still do almost everything she wants, but occasionally she asks me to open a package or a jar and then tells me how I have my father's hands. It's true, though sadly, after ninety years of use, his are seizing up, their joints swollen stiff. His grip is very weak now and he has a mysterious, distracting tingling in his palms—*not* carpal tunnel syndrome—which doctors are unable to diagnose or cure.

"Don't we have some *soft* butter?" he complains. We want to do things for him, but that makes him angry. He finds his own way—pushes his knife handle over the edge of the table in order to take hold of it, then slides the blade under his spoon to help him pick that up too. It takes time. He drops the knife, lifts his hands briefly toward his face, glares at them, lowers them onto the table where they lie, the fingers spread, surrounded by a scattering of crumbs. His nails have thickened and, neglected, grown long and irregular, none too clean. The cuticles likewise are overgrown. Long

---

[2] At that time no one had yet transplanted a hand. The first human hand transplant was carried out in 1999, and although the surgery went well, it was not ultimately a success: this transplant has turned out to be one of the most difficult to cope with psychologically. As Donna Dickenson puts it in *Body Shopping*: "It would take someone with a very firmly rooted sense of identity to cope with waking up every morning to find someone else's hand, a dead man's hand, peeping over the duvet."

white hairs sprout between the knuckles and the first finger joint. The skin is purplish on the knuckles, paper white and bluish on the backs of the hands, yellowing at the fingertips. These are hands very much in the unrelenting style of Stanley Spencer or Lucian Freud. One day, I expect, these will be "my" hands too.

"Well," he said, when we first measured and compared our hands, my child's version planted on top of his adult one, smaller, fresh looking, but structurally identical. "You could do worse. Suppose you had my ears!" His ears were large and hairy, and I was very glad not to have them. I used to slip my hand into his and feel its heat and vastness. He made things and fixed what the rest of us broke. But now, he sits in his place at the head of the oval dining table, cursing as he tries to get his breakfast to his mouth. His hands have failed him—and of all the pains and losses old age has brought, this is the one he feels most keenly—for, in some circles at least, a man, still, is what he can do and make.

A woman, though, is often caught up in how she looks and what she signifies. I have friends who, beginning a relationship, suffer agonies about their figure, their hair, or the texture of their skin, but in my case it was always because of my hands that I wanted to turn down the lights or to blindfold my lover: not every man is going to be happy to see what appear to be another man's hands caressing him. I can still feel that way now, after outdoor work, even though I've been married more than a decade.

As a girl, blissfully unaware of what my hands might mean, I used them to the full—not just for writing, drawing, and the like. I hung from the bars in the gym, climbed trees, kicked up my legs and walked upside down or cartwheeled, using my hands as feet. When another girl once exclaimed, in a horrified whisper, "Your hands! How big they are!" I held them up, widened my eyes, and growled back, "All the better to throttle you with!" Though really, they are not outright ugly or frightening—just rather unkempt and completely without feminine mystique or glamour of any kind.

When I met my husband, his hands, very well kept and deemed

by fellow cricketers to be *the safest pair of hands in the valley*, capable of catching almost anything a batsman could deliver, intrigued me from the start. I liked that they were elegant yet stronger than mine. I liked that, ever so gently, he would brush my palm with his fingers before he took hold.

"You and Daddy should hold hands more often," my ten-year-old son told me the other day. This would be difficult, since he still walks between us and occasionally takes one of our hands, or both, but I didn't tell him that: I want to delay, for as long as possible, the moment when he will stop doing so.

"Good idea!" I said. "I do like holding hands."

"Which way do you like best?" my daughter asked, shyly. At fourteen, she recently admitted to having a boyfriend. Her hands are long-fingered and elegant, more like my mother-in-law's than either my husband's or mine. My son, on the other hand, has that telltale extra-broad palm; even when he was very small, it was clear that he had "my" backward bending thumbs.

"Do you prefer it like this?" my daughter interlaced her fingers with mine. "Or the other way?"

I found it impossible to choose. "What about you?"

"This way," she said, interlaced still, squeezing very gently. "I like it this way."

A hand is difficult to separate and define, because it works only in intimate concert with other parts of the body. It's part of the arm, which in turn is related to the shoulder. It works in constant two-way communication with the brain, continuously modifying its supposed master even as it carries out its instructions to explore, to manipulate, or to practise to the point of perfection.

My father's attempt to pick up his knife involves his eyes, his nervous system, quite possibly his neck, as well as his brain, shoulder, arm, wrist, and only then the hand itself: palm, five digits, one of them an opposable thumb. It's because of our independently moving, finely adjustable fingers and very mobile, opposable thumbs that we can both grip and finely manipulate: wield scalpels, plait braids, shell peas, tie knots, pluck guitar strings or play the violin, turn a key in a lock, or pick up, sharpen, and then control a pencil. It's second nature for us to write our names, turn the page, decorate our pottery, take notes, to externalize our thoughts, sketch what we see or dream of.

To draw a hand, you need to understand what lies beneath the skin. It's one of the hardest forms to interpret: so many planes and angles, so much geometry, and at the same time, so much subtlety and gradation, texture and character. Leonardo could do it, and Dürer; the hand demands an artist of the very highest order. As for that hand of Michelangelo's, index finger outstretched—The Hand of God—it is for me an image of *human* agency and creativity, the whole of our creative intelligence and all that is good and bad in us brought to the finger's very tip.[3] I'm inclined to dismiss palmistry,[4] but I know that our fate and our hands are intimately connected— that, as a species, our hands have made us what we are, for better *and* for worse. We've always known this, and perhaps it is why hands appear, along with the beasts, in prehistoric cave paintings at Lascaux, Chauvet, and elsewhere.

Our hands feed our brains with information about the feel and weight of the world; they build intricate cultures and technologies. They have remade the world—to the point where many of us now live in a man-made, handmade world, unable to imagine what things would be like without us.

[3] If drawing someone else's hand is fiendishly difficult, using one hand to draw your other is harder still—disorientating, paradoxical. The etching "Drawing Hands," by M.C. Escher, sums up the situation.

[4] Though it does seem that our hands may turn out to be *somewhat* predictive of our fates: according to a recent study, there is a correlation between the relative length of men's index and ring fingers and their risk of contracting prostate cancer. Perhaps some arbitrary genetic linkage is involved—and if that is so, it's not impossible that character traits could, likewise, be associated with the shape and even the wrinkle patterns of the skin on the hands.

But our hands are only as good as the brains, beliefs, and hearts that propel them into action: they're also responsible for mass murder, atomic weaponry, and pollution on an enormous scale. They torture, they plunder, and while we *are* what our hands can do, they also stand in for us and for what we have done. Amnesty International reports that in countries where amputation is a judicial punishment, some of those hired by the state to carry out the sentence speak of the emotional difficulty they face in inflicting such a terrible physical, emotional, and symbolic loss. It is worse for them, they say, than carrying out an execution.

Not all hands are built the same way, and where one body part ends and another begins is open to debate, but there are approximately twenty-nine bones in a hand, a similar number of major joints, and one hundred and twenty-two ligaments. The fingers themselves contain no muscles: their movements are controlled by thirty-five muscles, of which seventeen are in the palm of the hand and eighteen in the forearm (these are the ones that hurt when you spend too long at the computer). There are thirty named arteries, forty-eight named nerves, which burgeon into an exquisite array at our fingertips—it's because of these that we can recognize a lover blindfolded, judge between silk and rayon, read Braille. As David Abram puts it in *Becoming Animal*, our hands are "two exceedingly tactile creatures."

The keeper of a pair of hands, unlike his or her social circle, sees them at work all day and knows them best—although those who live by their hands are also especially attuned to those of others. Musicians spend long hours perfecting the connection between hands, brain, and outer world, and so identify very strongly with not just their own, but also other people's hands; they feel a terrible blend of panic and sympathy at the mere mention of an injury or disease that would affect practice and performance. "Musicians' concern for their hands," Frank Wilson writes in *The Hand*, "is a by-product of the intense striving through which they turn them into the essential instrument for the realization of their own ideas or closely held feelings." In online forums, pianists discuss among themselves the qualities of the ideal hand (size, apparently, can be a disadvantage—long fingers are not necessarily a good thing), and according to *The Times*, the young Chinese virtuoso Lang Lang insures his hands for a seven-figure sum. But these are extremes. Most of us take our hands for granted—we are, to varying degrees oblivious of or even outright abusive to them—we are dependent on the multi-digited entities on the ends of our arms for almost everything we do—until, that is, they let us down.

My father's plate is empty, and my mother goes upstairs to dress for the day: we're going out later. I carry the breakfast things from the table to kitchen, where I mess about—cleaning the sink, then drying cutlery and replacing it in the drawer—so as to give Dad time. I know that he doesn't want me to watch his struggle to sign his name in the birthday card for Mum that waits, open, on the table, the pen propped ready beside it (a fat pen, supposedly easier to grip). It's important to him, to Mum, to me that, if possible, he writes his own name in the card. *Hand* also means handwriting. *In his hand*, we say (or used to say), meaning that the writer made the words on the page. He had a *good hand*.

A lovers' pledge or trial marriage is called a *handfast*, and the handfasting ceremony may involve the couple's right hands being literally tied together. Some people still choose to commit themselves to each other this way, even though it's no longer legally recognized. *Hand* is also a verb, meaning to pass to someone, or to assist them. *Hand* (the noun again) can also stand in for the whole person—or at least, his capacity for work—as in *hired hand*, or "All hands on deck!" Hands are absolutely everywhere in our language (which, it has been argued, they, and not the tongue, vocal chords, and lips, are responsible for creating in the first place). They have demanded their own verbs: clench, grasp, stroke, twist, squeeze, wring, clutch, flex, press, pluck, caress, and punch, to name but a few . . . The specialized movements of our hands make up our lives: knitting, typing, tying, sewing, stirring. And the imagery of the hand peppers our speech: hand in hand, we say, on hand, hands down, on the other hand, second hand, hands on, hand in glove, hand in hand, handed on, even-handed, heavy-handed, high-handed, empty-handed, hand-me-down, hand over fist . . .

Every culture's proverbs are littered with references to the hand. "The fingers of the same hand are not alike," they say in Portugal. "Without fingers," they say in Morocco, "the hand would be a spoon." In Africa, the question is, "Shall we kill a snake and carry it in our hand, when we have a bag for putting long things in?"

We talk of someone as being a handful, or of losing his grip on a situation, of burning his fingers, of forcing another person's hand, or giving them a free hand, or a handout; of lending a hand or of being heavy-handed; we say that someone has played into our hands. Give me a hand! we yell up the stairs. The idea took hold of him, we say. It would not let go of him (or vice versa). We crave first-hand knowledge. We speak of someone as grasping—meaning greedy—or say that they have grasped an idea. We observe that the left hand does not know what the right is doing, or notice that so-and-so is living from hand to mouth; we long to wash our hands of a problem, thirst to take the law into our own hands, struggle to get the upper hand. Some of us have roving hands, and, when looking for a sexual encounter, we might pick someone up. And a hand is also a set of cards, hence the chance we are given in life—and we play our hand as best we can, or we show it. We try to keep our hand in; we long to win hands down. Some of us have blood on our hands. We speak of greasing a bureaucrat's palm, of the iron fist in the velvet glove, of being manipulated. One hand, we say, washes the other . . . Hand it over, we say. Get a grip, and let's pick up where we left off.

The world is indeed at our fingertips, though these days work, for many, is tapping at the keyboard, a terrible waste of our hands' infinite repertoire. Software designers are trying to eliminate that too. Perhaps we'll soon be able to talk into our machines, and knit, embroider, or massage each other while we write. But it seems to me that the mind-to-hand, hand-to-word connection is a necessary, almost holy thing.[5] My handwriting sprawls, increasingly eccentric, and, to begin with, my hand resists the effort of forming the letters, rebels and cramps, somehow allowing my mind to veer sideways and escape. But still, I like to make my words this way. I like to be alone with the whisper of the pencil on the page, my eyes watching the line form one shape to the next.

Long ago, during the Second World War, my father penned hundreds of letters to my mother, which she kept; recently, with both parents' permission, I read them. Dad's writing was smaller than mine is, more restrained; the letter shapes, and the ways of linking them, quite different from those I was taught. But I see a similarity in the way we put words on the page: a certain lack of care for the taught form, a hurtling, hurried look that comes from badly wanting to say what's in our hearts and minds. We both leave plenty of space between words and between lines, as if to allow our words to breathe.

Now, he squares up to each letter of his name, forms them one by one, with a small rest in between. For all the effort, the writing is ghostly, as if the ink has barely grazed the page. But when he wrote to my mother, my father's hands were strong and lean, his nails clean and neatly filed; he wrote unhindered, pouring his thoughts onto the page. I know, from the letters themselves, how, at the beginning of his five-year journey, the noise and vibration of the troop ship's engine was transmitted through every surface and fitting, even the clipboard on his lap and the pen itself (a fountain pen, at the beginning of the war—later, in the desert, it was a pencil stub). "Darling, my handwriting is terrible. The ship makes it shake. Forgive me. I have been remembering how you . . . ." He recounted his daily life, skating over the combat side of things. He remembered caressing my mother. He sent poems, written after brief home leaves, and wrapped up packets of stockings and bolts of silk to mail back home. Writing was a small respite from the work of the

---

[5] Norman Doidge argues, in *The Brain That Changes Itself*, that writing by hand is, at the very least, a kind of workout for our brains.

war: his hands also fired a small automatic rifle called a Bren gun, and heavy artillery too. They dismantled mines, repaired trucks, and improvised equipment out of scraps of metal and wire.

After his return, there were no more letters. A postcard, perhaps, if he was away on business. He wrote at work: columns of figures, notes, reports, and speeches. He moved into increasingly managerial roles and even had a secretary to type out his dictation, but at home, he built sheds, laid paving stones, cut dovetail joints, serviced cars, lawnmowers, and bikes, and would approach an especially awkward repair with what seemed like relish. He signed himself *Love, Dad* at the end of letters my mother wrote to me.

It's possible to live without hands; the part of our brains that deals with their input will, if pushed, accept it from elsewhere. For my father, though, that transition is impossible. I slide the card into its envelope, and then, because doing something with my hands is how I respond to both sadness and rage, I go to the bathroom and rummage through overstuffed drawers and cabinets and unearth eventually—from among the stockpiles of never-to-be-used hotel soaps and shampoos, the E45 cream, safety pins, and carefully rolled elastic bandages—a pair of not-too-blunt nail scissors, a nail clipper, and an ancient file.

When I suggest the manicure, Dad takes a moment or two to study the arid, confusing handscape, blotched, hairy, divided by blue-back veins.

"Not pretty," he says, looking up. "And it's not a task your mother enjoys. Go ahead . . . The fact is," he adds, "she needs new glasses, but she won't listen to me on that score."

We migrate slowly to the lounge. I gather a tray, a towel, a face flannel, a tub of the E45 cream, and a bowl of warm water. It's going to work best with him in the armchair and me on my knees.

"Music?"

He nods. I press the switch, take his left hand, and press it between my two. "Cold!" I tell him, rubbing it between mine.

He shrugs: it doesn't bother him, he can hardly feel the damn things anymore. I hold his thumb still while I try the scissors, abandon them in favour of the clippers. Soon, fragments ping across the room. As Dad drifts off to sleep, I file the corners of his nails smooth, soak each hand in warm water, dry them, massage with moisturizer. It strikes me that I'm using the hands he passed to me to groom the hands that mine will become.

"Your father is not the man I married," Mum tells me. Her bold handwriting with its loops and flourishes is unaltered. She's very much in control of her life and proud of it too.

"He really is not." She sips her coffee. The wedding ring glows, clean and bright on her finger. "He sleeps like this half the day. It's not fun." Mum has been saying these kinds of things to me and my sisters for some time now. None of us wants to hear them.

"But he's still connected to that man, isn't he?" I try to put the case: he's not the exact same man who went to the war and wrote those love letters, just as she isn't the same woman who received them. But he's not *completely* different. The new self has evolved from the old, and he still cares for her very much, which seems to me to be an immense treasure, though that's not how it feels to Mum.

"He can't *do* anything," she tells me. The division of manual labour between my parents was always the old-fashioned one, in which he took responsibility for things requiring strength, technical know-how, or the use of serious tools of any kind, and she sewed, cooked, put in bedding plants, and pulled out weeds.

"I've already grieved for him," Mum says. She sits very still for a few moments, her hands in her lap, looking ahead. Then she turns to me, says, "And really—what is there to celebrate in a birthday now?"

All the same, I have tickets for a Gilbert and Sullivan matinee, and despite her doubts, we set off; I help lever Dad into the taxi, steer us into the theatre. When a man in a big coat sits in front of us, blocking Mum's view, she stretches forward and briskly folds down his collar. Feeling her touch, he spins around, but once he has understood, he does not seem to mind. The lights dim and the many-fingered orchestra starts up; ten minutes into the show, my mother and father exchange a glance and, as the theatre fills with laughter, she reaches for his hand, pulls it onto her lap, and settles her smaller one loosely on top of it. Slowly, then, as if driving some kind of fleshy crane, my father brings his other hand over. It hovers, descends, then twice, clumsily, he strokes her hand from fingers to wrist before enveloping it with his. It's possible that I imagine the almost imperceptible squeeze that follows, as my parents look back toward the brightly lit stage.

So I'm proud to have my father's hands. And while hands are both powerful extensions (and creators) of the self, to my mind, the most important thing about them is not their role in agency and ingenuity, technology and creativity, but the way they connect us— the repertoires of gesture (consider, for example, how our hands can amplify or undercut our words, or, in sign languages, entirely replace them), and of touch.

Sometimes our hands connect us formally, as when we shake or kiss them, or ceremonially, when they may impart a blessing, make a promise, mark an agreement, or slip on (or receive) a wedding ring. We join hands in political solidarity—a collective gesture that says we are one, and together we will not be broken. Our hands join us in comfort, *in extremis*, or in passionate desire, when words fail. One set of exquisitely sensitive nerves presses against another, sensing the permeability of the skin that separates it from its counterpart, the flow of blood beneath, the electricity of one nervous system yearning to merge with another. Fingers interlace, stroke. Palms brush, press together, and the body ignites. Sometimes, holding hands is the only thing to do; it may also be the best thing we ever do. As parents, hand in hand with our children, we feel the utter sweetness of our task; in caring for someone who is sick, we move beyond words, let our hands do what is needed. In death, we finally let go, and our hands are placed by the hands of others over our heart, open, inward, empty, resting at last.

Pas de Deux

Dede Crane

When I was walking that fading line between childhood and womanhood, my mother's critical eye was often focused on me.

"If you must cross your legs, keep your knees together and cross your ankles."

"When having your picture taken, angle your body forty-five degrees and place one foot"—the downstage foot—"slightly forward of the other."

"Brush your knees together when you walk."

This last suggestion requires a small push from the toe to lift and smooth one bony knee past the other, which causes the hips to sway, with subtlety, from side to side. This walk is not just lovely and feminine but downright seductive. Only now do I realize that her instructions were equivalent to a lioness teaching hunting tips to her cub: they were to help me attract a mate.

There was nothing delicate about my mother's beauty: Penny Crane was five-foot-ten, slender but large-boned, with man-sized hands and size ten feet. Before having her three children, she wore an eight and a half shoe, claiming her feet grew a half-size during each pregnancy. With the onset of her labours, she refused to head to the hospital until she'd shaved her legs and painted her toenails. That was her birth plan, her prenatal prep. It didn't matter that she was to be given a general anesthetic and knocked out for the event. She was perfectly content to be kept in the dark about what went on *down there*. What she did know was that her legs and feet were going to be exposed to her doctor and handled by strangers.

My mother's devotions to beauty were not founded on a surreptitious need to keep up appearances; they were founded on a simple desire to make the world a more physically beautiful place in whatever way she could, big or small. A successful interior designer and watercolourist, she had a well-trained and critical eye.

My mother wore tan leather pants in her sixties and wore them well. She had permanent eyeliner tattooed on her eyelids in her seventies to save herself the trouble. She never allowed herself to go grey, not even on her deathbed. During the last year of her life, whenever she was coming to or leaving the hospital, no matter how ill, she would take the time to choose her outfit, her earrings and rings, make sure her hair was in place, put on the right colour lipstick, and, finally, her oversized sunglasses. As I wheeled her down the hall, her knees together and chin proud, heads would inevitably do a double take wondering if she just might be somebody famous or, at the very least, rich.

I began ballet lessons at the age of five at the local public school gym. I was the kid who could lie on her stomach with the soles of her feet together and pelvis flat on the ground, froglike, while the other little bums rode up in the air like grasshoppers.

"She has natural turnout," the teacher told my mom. This referred to my hip rotation. "And musicality. You should consider sending her to a professional school."

At the National Ballet in Washington, DC, I took classes twice a week, which eventually became three times a week. I was on pointe by age ten, the shoes like bricks on the end of my skinny legs, and was proud to show Mom my blood-stained tights after each class. My second toe, being longer than my big toe, was constantly blistered at the first joint, a joint that eventually became permanently buckled. I learned to nightly paint my toes with Mercurochrome, which stained them a vivid candy apple red and was supposed to toughen up the skin against blisters. Toenails were kept short and cut with a dip in the centre in order to avoid them becoming ingrown. To keep my leg muscles supple, I wrapped my legs with rags soaked in castor oil.

At thirteen, I auditioned for and was accepted into a performing arts high school called The Academy of the Washington Ballet. There I trained three hours a day and attended academic classes. The maximum number of students I ever had in my grade was a whopping ten. At fourteen, I went on a thousand-calorie-a-day grapefruit diet and lost twenty pounds. Just shy of five-foot-eight, I went from one hundred and thirty-five pounds to one hundred and fifteen, eventually dropping to one hundred and ten. My period magically disappeared and didn't reappear for nearly a decade. The following year, at a school party, several classmates taught me the art of throwing up. Fingers, chopstick, or raw egg? Always lots of water.

My mother called me Twiggy and thought I looked sensational. I thought so too.

Soon, I could press my stomach flat to the ground while my legs did a complete side splits and my toes pointed at the ceiling. I could bite my own toenails, put both feet behind my head. I could place my heel in my hand and straighten that leg over my head, then let go without it moving. To my mother's dismay, the more flexible I became the harder it was to sit, stand, or walk with my knees together.

In summers I trained in Manhattan, on scholarship, and in Saratoga Springs, where I first met my mentor, Melissa Hayden.

Formerly Mildred Herman of Toronto, Melissa began studying ballet at the absurdly late age of fourteen, became a prima ballerina of the New York City Ballet, and was the lightning-footed "stunt" dancer in the movie *The Red Shoes*. She was considered short for one of Balanchine's dancers, all ribcage and legs, legs, legs, which, rumour had it, had been insured for one hundred thousand dollars apiece. Melissa was not a beautiful woman by any standard—until she stepped on a stage.

Because of Melissa, I left high school after Grade 11 with an equivalency degree and moved to Saratoga to study with her full-time. Unlike the other teachers I'd trained with, Melissa connected the dots between one step and the next. She broke down the mechanics of movement and put them back together in a way that spoke directly to the body. In other words, she taught movement, not steps, and, beyond that, the difference between possessing technique and being an artist.

I remember the time she was making her rounds as we did our grand battements—large kicks—at the barre. She stopped alongside me and I began to shake inside.

"Put your eyes in your feet," she said over the music. Melissa's voice was all Mildred: tough, nasal, and overtly Jewish.

What? I continued to brush my foot along the floor and throw my leg skyward to the beat of the music, desperate to get it right and impress her.

"They're smarter than this." She pointed to my head, made googly eyes in my face.

Not understanding, I looked at her sideways, my eyes asking, begging the ques—

"Like pearls to swine," she muttered and moved on.

Ballet, according to Melissa, started and ended with the feet. Ninety-nine per cent of the language of ballet translates to the actions and angles of the legs and feet. Plié is to bend at the hips, knees, and ankles, relevé to rise up on the toes, passé to pass the feet over the knee, sauté to jump, frappé to strike the floor with the ball of the foot, fouetté to whip the leg, developpé to unfold the leg skyward, and on and on.

Millie urged us to practise picking up marbles with our metatarsus—the ball of our foot. "Your feet should feel like hands," she said, and they did.

My feet became the most sentient part of my body. They drew the music's notes and lines on the stage floor and through the air like sign language. The reach and pull of my feet drove one leg downward, the strongest of stems, and suspended the other weightless in the air in a passé or arabesque. Dancing, I expressed my feelings through my feet first, my face second.

When Melissa accepted a position on the other coast, I auditioned for her company and at the age of seventeen moved across country and began my professional career.

I developed bunions the size of garlic bulbs, the pain of which turned Motrin into candy. The zinging pain of shin splints as the ligaments criss-crossing up the leg were lifted away from the bone, combined with stress fractures in both my tibia and fibula, put me on crutches once a year. These injuries were temporarily corrected by ultrasound and by flexing my ankles with a weighted purse strapped over my toes.

Melissa did not get on with management and was eventually fired. I and other devotees left in protest. After a six-month stint as a soloist in Chicago, I returned to New York's Upper West Side, this time as a principal dancer in a company across the river. One night I was at a party in the Chelsea loft of Susan, one of my fellow company members. Susan, a few years older, had been with the company for a lot longer than I had yet remained in the corps de ballet. We were friends, so I thought, when, that night she stumbled up to me, clearly drunk. "How come," she said, "your legs are so fucking long?"

Not realizing this was a rhetorical question, I started to say that her legs were probably just as long when she told me she hated me and poured the remains of her drink on the floor, splattering our legs equally.

There is nothing wrong with the artistic aesthetic of ballet, however narrow and physically demanding. The problem is that it is an art that depends on young bodies, and those bodies are stronger than the young minds they house, minds that, like toes, can buckle under pressure. By the time I was twenty, I understood the damage I was doing to myself. I quit shortly thereafter.

Two years before my mother died, she flew from Washington, DC, to take a trip with me, my husband, and our four kids to Puerto Vallarta, Mexico. The long plane ride caused her feet to swell, and they remained so for her entire two-week visit. She could fit into only one pair of shoes, sandals that required buckling, and could not put them on without my help. I remember walking the streets of downtown Puerto Vallarta, her arm depending on my arm as we hunted down slip-ons that would satisfy her taste. We went from one open-air shoe store to another, where, with no success, I carefully slipped pair after pair onto her bloated, skin-stretched feet.

Once back home, my mother was diagnosed with congestive heart failure. The weakened heart's inability to circulate fluids properly first shows up in the body part farthest from the heart: the feet. Medication was, initially, able to reduce the swelling, but it soon returned and began its slow ascent. First to her ankles. Then to her knees. Then above her knees. No amount of diuretics or change of heart medication made any lasting difference. Her swollen skin became hard and painful to the touch. It turned dry and scaly, blackening in places until the skin began to split and bleed. One leg began to "weep," as the doctor termed it. It wept enough tears to soak her pant leg and require a towel beneath her chair to protect the carpet. Soon the second one was weeping too. I wrapped her legs in layers of absorbent pads and gauze, which would soak through in a matter of an hour, maybe two. The best and easiest solution, my sister discovered, was wrapping both legs in adult-sized diapers. Blisters the size of fists formed on the sides and back of her calves and tops of her feet, like something out of a crude science fiction novel.

My mother hid her unattractive legs as best she could. Shoes were now replaced with thick socks. When one of the blisters popped, it left behind raw, red patches, no different than if the epidermis had been peeled back or burned away. The largest and most dramatic blister was the one that hitched a ride on the top of her left foot, covering the entire size-ten surface. Its smooth dome and size reminded me of a snow globe. Only the liquid in this snow globe was an opaque gold. It was more fascinating to me than ugly, and in a strange way, I might even say it was beautiful. After days of watching it grow and make its self-satisfied home there on her foot, my mother—who never entirely lost her sense of humour—and I decided it deserved a name. We called it Goldie.

After a week, Goldie finally popped—though only partially—and infection set in. The pain was defeating.

After I ended my ballet career, I went to university, but I continued to make my living through dance: teaching and, on occasion, performing, off my toes, with various contemporary companies. While working as a ballet instructor, choreographer, and artistic director of Dance Fredericton in New Brunswick, I learned that legs could predict the sex of one's child.

It was a friend, a mother of six, who'd passed along this particular old wives' tale. If pregnant with a girl, I was told, the hair on your legs grew at a snail's pace. When pregnant with a boy, leg hair grew like an ape's. The theory, supposedly hormone-based, proved absolutely true for my future four pregnancies—two of each sex—and I have asked the shaving question of many mothers-to-be since and believe the results are worthy of a science journal article or two.

Like most mothers, I marvelled at my babies' feet and, though not wishing a ballet career on any of them, could not help but think of Fernando Bujones. The feet of this former star with New York's American Ballet Theatre were famous among dancers and balletomanes. As a rule, males don't have much arc to the top of their feet, and therefore the dramatic aesthetic line of the leg is left to the women. Fernando was the exception. His mother was a ballet dancer, as was his grandmother, and they both spent hours each day massaging the malleable bones of his newborn feet, sculpting them like clay into their vision of the perfect, history-making pointe.

I was just shy of forty when back trouble coupled with fibromyalgia ended my thirty-five-year affair with dance. My feet survived relatively intact. The calluses have faded, the buckled joints are notable only by feel, and the bunions are smaller and pain-free thanks to expensive insoles in my shoes. I mourned the loss of expressing myself in movement, and I still see patterns of dance when a piece of music hits a certain visceral chord. Needing a new creative outlet, I gradually turned to another kind of storytelling, writing fiction. Dance was my first emotional language, English my second, and the part of the brain responsible for dancing with words felt, and probably looked like, my big toe after an hour's soak in the bath. In those early writing years, after long bouts struggling with the steps and the flow of rhythmic prose, my brain would literally ache. Not like a headache, more like a sorely underused muscle.

Three days before my mother died, she had her blond hair washed and cut by a friend of my sister's who came to the house. It was a good cut. When the priest, a young man in his mid-thirties, came to the house to administer the last rights, he stopped short in her bedroom doorway.

"My, you are a beautiful woman," he said. It was not merely an objective statement, I thought, it was if he'd understood her.

If only you could have seen me in my day, her eyes seemed to say, her voice having gone to wherever voices go. And then, under the sheet, she slowly but surely shifted one knee over to touch the other.

When my mother died, I believed the world had lost the last of the great glamourpusses—it would now be a less beautiful place. In the weeks that followed, I felt as though I'd become untethered from the earth. I couldn't wrap my brain around where she was, where she'd gone, or the ridiculous fact that she wasn't ever coming back. An essential part of me, I believe, had gone off in search of her. I cried all the time, required the constant reassurance of physical touch, and fell asleep each night staring at the towering cedar outside our bedroom window, clinging to the idea of its roots being as deep as the tree was tall. During the day I walked. Compulsively. I walked for miles, never wanting to stop, needing to pound the earth with my feet, force my breath in and out and propel my legs forward, right, left, right, left, in an even rhythm. Some instinct understood that in order to get beyond the sense of loss and of feeling lost, I had to put my eyes in my feet, use my legs and walk there.

vagina,
penis,
womb,
breasts,
ass . . .

My Vagina
André Alexis

On "Vagina"

I first *almost* saw a woman's pudendum at the age of eleven. One of my father's friends, on the occasion of his marriage, surrendered his collection of *Playboy*s to me. The gift was meant as a "joke," but I received some ten or twenty magazines whose industrially sweet smell and glossy feel I still remember. They were taken away from me, weeks later, when someone—my mother, I guess—felt that the "joke" had gone on long enough. The *Playboy*s had had their effect by then, though. I had developed a slight obsession with tan lines, a desire for white skin, and an abiding curiosity about the inevitably obscured—hidden by animal fur or cushions or bales of hay—montes pubis of the young women photographed for the magazine. It was not until a few years later that *Playboy* began to show the vulvas of its models, by which time the magazine began to arouse something more than my instincts, though the carefulness of the photography became cloying—if you can use that word about images—and sometimes off-putting.

For years, I thought that the mons pubis was what is meant by the word *vagina*. One of the consequences of this confusion is that I find shaved pudenda unattractive, a kind of bewildering nonsignifier. Even now, when I've been physically proximate to a number of women's pudenda, I'm likely to say "vagina" when what I mean is "mons pubis" or "vulva." In short, the distinction between vulva and vagina is relatively recent for me and not absolute. And I've sometimes wondered just what the consequences of this misalliance (vagina, vulva) have been for my psyche and my "sexual self," a self conditioned by fashion photography and mercantile interests.

Actually . . . I was once chided for using the phrase "hair on a vagina." My partner had had enough of my confusing *vulva*—the visible part of female genitalia—and *vagina*—the canal that leads from the vulva to the womb. Was I not a doctor's son? Saying *vulva* when you mean *vagina* is akin to saying *lips* when you mean *throat*, yeah? So, *stop* it already. I was suitably chastened, but . . . the confusion of the two words is fairly common and revealing. For instance, I recently watched a harrowing documentary titled *The Perfect Vagina*. It was made for Channel 4 in England by Lisa Rogers. Rogers was upset by the rise in labioplasties in England. Labioplasty is the procedure whereby the labia minora or labia majora are cut—one is tempted to write *amputated*—if they are deemed too "big" or too "floppy." At one point in the documentary, Rogers says, "I think I'd be horrified, absolutely horrified if, in fifteen years' time [my daughter] came to me and said, 'I don't like the way my vagina looks.'" Rogers immediately corrects herself, changing it to "I don't like the way my *vulva* looks." But, in fact, hers is a minor slip. The documentary itself should have been called *The Perfect Vulva*, as the subject is plastic surgery on the vulva. Even more interesting: while individuals often confound *vulva* and *vagina*, so does our language. *Vulva* is, in fact, the Latin word for "womb" or "vagina." (*Vagina* itself being a Latin word that means "sheath" or "scabbard.") So, at one point, *vulva* referred to the hidden, not the visible. The word suffered a sea change on its journey to English. Now, few people would confound *lips* with *throat*, but *vulva* and *vagina* are a fated pair. Though we would like a word, a *single* word, for female genitalia, we need two: one for the hidden aspect and one for the visible.

(It's been suggested that the word *cunt* refers to both the visible and the hidden, and I like that idea because I like the word. It's such a pleasure to say. However, in Canada, *cunt* is deeply offensive and is most often used as an insult or as a thoughtless put-down. For instance, in advertising parlance, televised ads that feature two women talking about a product—dish soap, say, or laundry detergent—are so common that they're referred to as "two c's in a k," that is, "two cunts in a kitchen," even when the ad isn't set in a kitchen. So, for my money, *cunt* is too diffuse a word to serve any specific purpose. The word *yoni* does refer to the female genitals as a whole, but in North America the word is associated with the Vedantic or the sacred. This association makes it too particular for everyday use. For example, a documentary titled *The Perfect Yoni* would almost certainly have to deal with Eastern notions of the sacred. Then again, words such as *pussy, poonanee,* or *poum poum*—which refer to the vulva or the vagina or both—are vulgar and somewhat infantile. So, they don't quite suit the purpose.)

Reflecting on the idea I had formed of the vagina, I'm reminded of John Ruskin, who, legend has it, was enchanted with his young bride until their wedding night when the reality of her vulva upset him so much that he could not consummate their marriage. This has always struck me as an interesting story, not because I understand why Ruskin was put off—I have never been "put off" in this way—but because I wonder what image he had made for himself of a vulva before encountering his young wife's particulars. He was a visual man, a decent enough watercolourist for J.W. Turner to have commented favourably on one of his sketches. So, he must have held in his mind some aesthetic-Platonic version of the vagina or vulva that his young wife's body did not meet. The difference between Ruskin's situation and ours is that both men *and* women of my generation were aware of *Playboy* or were familiar with the models therein. So, for a time, men were more likely than not to encounter the trimmed vulvas the magazine had led them to expect.

I've obviously been ignoring class and economic differences, up to this point. Writer Alan Moore has pointed out that *Hustler* was a magazine for lower-class men while *Playboy* was for the middle class. The distinction between "erotic" (i.e., *Playboy*) and "pornographic" (i.e., *Hustler*) was, thus, at least in part, a class distinction. Because the magazines presented vulvas in different ways, it follows that the vagina or vulva I've so far referred to is a socio-economic phenomenon, a socio-economic "creation." The vagina is constructed, for men born in the mid-twentieth century, in a way it could not have been for Ruskin. I mean, it is difficult— *very* difficult—to imagine a man of our time who had not seen photographs of a vulva before happening upon his wife's or first girlfriend's pudendum. A man of Ruskin's time (and class) would have had to go out of his way—even if not *that* far—to see such photographs. I don't think our experience gives us an unarguable advantage over the men of the nineteenth century. Any number of men from my socio-economic class (and time) may have been "put off" actual pudenda by exposure to the "*Playboy* pudendum." So, no doubt, some of the scorn I've heard expressed for Ruskin's naïveté—as if unavoidable visual experience of each other's sexual organs has made us less hung-up sexually—is hypocritical.

I mention all of these things because I want to insist on the created-ness of the vagina I'm writing about here, its mixture of the sexually fascinating, the socially created (I'm middle class), and the utterly particular (I'm writing of the vagina from the perspective of *my* five senses). It's the intersection of instinct, culture, and the senses that interests me, and I'm not certain how much any of this will mean to a reader who does not share my origins or class, my gender or sexual orientation.

1. On Taste
The taste of a vagina is notoriously difficult to describe. In my experience, it's slightly salty, sea-tinged (to be specific: the Mediterranean, off the coast of Italy, some time in the year 2000). But then again . . . no, not really or not always. It depends on the woman, on the time of month, or the time of day. It depends on the woman's diet. And on her state of arousal. There's a kind of "brightness" to the taste of a vagina's secretions just before orgasm. (I know *brightness* is not quite right, but is there another word for the journey from viscosity to clarity, a "clarity" in both texture *and* taste?) ·

One sometimes hears the tang of a vagina compared to that of cheese or fish. These are clichés and, to me, they're way off. More intriguing comparisons, comparisons closer to my experience because more subtle, include blood, copper pennies, truffles, brown butter, almonds, melon, lemon, durian, rain in a forest, an Amaretto sour (¾ oz. lemon juice, sugar, 1½ oz. Amaretto), the aftertaste of V8, fresh oysters . . .

I recently read that vagina-as-flavour is rather like the taste left in the mouth after one has put both connectors of an almost dead nine-volt battery on one's tongue: slightly metallic. Now, this turned out to be surprisingly *true*. I mean, having conducted the experiment—having put the nine-volt connectors on my tongue—I found that, yes, there's something to this. I recognized the taste. In this I am, apparently, far from alone. Strange to think of a battery as having a "delicate taste," but as I associate the taste of vagina with a certain delicacy . . .

(A nine-volt battery contains manganese dioxide, powdered zinc, potassium hydroxide, and brass. Is there something in one of these elements or the combination of them that approximates the taste of a woman aroused?)

Curiously, this speculation brings Trinidad, the country of my birth, to mind. There—and elsewhere in the Caribbean—there is a thing called "sweat rice." It is made by a woman who wants to capture the affection of a man or one who wants to retain the affection of a husband she fears is straying. In effect, sweat rice is a love potion, and it's done like this: the woman makes rice. Then, while the rice is still steaming, she stands over a bowl of the rice so that the steam from the rice bathes her vagina. The resultant juices fall into the rice. And so you have sweat rice, also known as "man yuh mus" or "man, you must." Any man who eats the sweat rice of a woman will be helplessly drawn to her. So, it's rather important that the *right* man eat the rice in question.

One can imagine a worse meal. I mean, how bad could it be to be eating stewed chicken with rice and then taste, *unexpectedly* taste, an Amaretto sour or copper pennies? That is, the unpleasant part would not be the taste so much as the too late realization that you were about to fall helplessly in love with your dinner companion. But as with all of these potions or magical means to keep a man (or a woman), sweat rice does bring up an unavoidable "why?" Affection captured by betrayal is bound to be second rate, isn't it?

(An aside: I've called "sweat rice" a "love potion" of sorts, and it is that, but it may also be used by those who are *not* in love with the objects of their attentions. In Tobago, I was told of a woman whose daughter and son-in-law lived in the same house as she did. When the daughter died, the son-in-law stayed in the house, helping his mother-in-law out. As the woman grew older and less able to do physically demanding things for herself, she became afraid that her son-in-law would leave. So, in the lunches she made for him every afternoon, there was inevitably a portion of sweat rice. One afternoon, he returned early for lunch and found his mother-in-law squatting over a bowl of rice. Though he was not the brightest of men, he knew immediately what she was up to and was disgusted. He left her home very soon afterwards, though she pleaded with him and swore she would never make sweat rice for him again.)

The most unusual thing about sweat rice, however, is its confluence of culture and intimacy. To my mind, anyway, this most secret and ineffable thing—the taste of a woman's vaginal secretions—is an entirely unexpected part of cultural discourse. It seems odd that a culture should have a *use* for vaginal secretions. And yet . . . not so odd. In Trinidad, spiderwebs were used to treat cuts and bruises long before it was discovered that spiderwebs contain a coagulant that helps stop bleeding. Somewhere, someone has no doubt done something theoretically efficacious with sweat or dried skin, saliva or urine.

There's something uncanny about the farther reaches of knowledge.

Well, I say "knowledge," but, of course, one wonders if sweat rice actually works. One wonders if the steam from the rice wouldn't be painful for the woman. One wonders who first thought of this procedure and who was the first "object of affection" (a Trinidadian?), and if he—or she—responded in the desired way immediately or only after getting to know the one who'd contrived to "sweat" into the rice. The particular circumstances of that first sweat rice must have been desperate, surreal, and in my imagination they are enduringly odd.

(A further note on Tobago. While I was living in Buccoo Point, I was told of another use for vaginal secretions. This use is called "butter breast." It is less a "love potion" than a means of control. To make butter breast, a woman rubs her vaginal secretions on her nipples so that, during love making, the man will take them in while kissing her breasts. I was assured that a man—once he tastes butter breast—will be more easily controlled by the woman whose secretions he's tasted.)

2. On Smell
Germaine Greer once wrote of the supposed aphrodisiac properties of vaginal secretions. She described dabbing a bit of the musk from her vagina behind her ear—I think it was—or betwixt her breasts. Men, she said, are instinctively drawn to the smell of vaginal secretions.

As with sweat rice, you can't help but wonder how *true* Greer's words are. Is this instinctive attraction the case for all men, hetero and homosexual? Does this work whatever the physical characteristics of the woman who's dabbed herself with this "musk"? If the vagina secretes a pheromone, can that pheromone be used for social or antisocial ends? (What, one wonders, would be its effect on a crowd of protesters? Pacification by aggressive distraction or incitement to aggression? Would it be useful to the police or to anarchists?)

I think most people would accept that the musk of a vagina—applied wherever you like—will only entice if the "muskee" (male or female) is inclined to appreciate the "musker's" other qualities, not just her scent. Still, this is an intriguing question—well, intriguing to me, anyway—because there is now a commercially sold scent called Vulva Original that purports to be the smell of a young blond woman's vaginal secretions.

(Note the misnomer. The vulva has no particular scent, the vagina does. So, why is the scent not marketed as Vagina Original?)

The head of the German company that sells Vulva Original is Guido Lenssen. He was interviewed by Saul Pullivan for *Vice* magazine. The interview is brief, and the questions were not particularly serious. A few of Lenssen's answers, however, were revealing. In answer to the question "Can you confirm that there is real vagina in [the scent]?" Lenssen said:

> Almost everything on the sex market is based on fantasy. The toys are plastic, the movies use actors. *Vulva* is real. We tried several samples from women of all ages. We didn't take the scent after someone had run a marathon or anything, but it is a combination of urine, sweat, and female arousal.

When asked about the "range of women" used, whether the scent is from one woman or several, Lenssen answered:

> [We used] one. She's the blond woman on our website. Of course, we wanted to take the scent from a woman that looks nice, but we tried with a variety of women as it was ultimately smell based, not about looks . . . I think when you smell it you will know it comes from a young woman.

There are obvious tergiversations in Guido Lenssen's answers. First, if Vulva Original is about smell, not looks, why should Lenssen insist on the blond woman whose scent was the basis for the musk? If the scent is specific to the young blonde on Vulva Original's website, would Vulva Original appeal to men who are attracted to non-blond, older women? (Are the vaginal secretions of older women actually identifiable as "older"?) Later in the interview, Lenssen states that Vulva Original is not meant as a perfume but, rather, as an enhancement to sex play or masturbation. It is, then, an aid to the imagination, a stimulus to fantasy. If so, isn't it rather closer to the sex toys and movie actors Lenssen described as fantastic?

In fact, it doesn't take much thought to understand that Vulva Original is entirely about fantasy and marketing. If the scent of vaginal secretions were genuinely aphrodisiac, there would be no need at all to insist that Vulva Original had come from a woman who looks nice. Exposure to the scent would arouse. Un point, ç'est tout. Guido Lenssen has to control the fantasy in order to sell it. So, the blonde on the company's homepage is scantily clad. She's in high heels. Her breasts are visible through a sheer, black top. She is naked from the waist down and faces the onlooker, legs apart, but she holds the bottle of Vulva Original in front of her vulva, obscuring the view. The company's motto? "The intimate smell of an irresistible woman."

Both sweat rice and Vulva Original are versions of what Sir James Frazer called "contagious magic." In *The Golden Bough*, Frazer defines contagious magic as a version of sympathetic magic that "proceeds upon the notion that things which have once been conjoined must remain ever afterwards, even when quite dissevered from each other, in such a sympathetic relation that whatever is done to the one must similarly affect the other." In the case of sweat rice, I suppose one could characterize the[6] logic in this way:

---

[1] This, the exact centre of my essay, seems as good a place as any to talk about the clitoris. The Latin word for clitoris (*landica*) was considered *extremely* vulgar. Even such writers as Catullus or Martial—scabrously frank, both of them—only alluded to the word, though Martial did write about a woman with a clitoris large enough to satisfy her lesbian lover. The question naturally arises: why should mention of the clitoris have been thought more vulgar than mention of the vulva (*cunnus*) or the penis (*mentula*)? Is it precisely *because*, for Roman men, the clitoris could be considered a small "phallus" and so was, in

having once tasted the secretions of a woman's vagina, the beloved cannot leave the woman. They are, as Frazer has it, conjoined. In the case of Vulva Original (interesting name, no?), the thought isn't about simple arousal. It's about that blonde. It's that the smell of the *irresistible woman*'s vagina will bring her in all her irresistibility to the one who has dabbed a bit of the pale yellow potion on his fingers or wrist.

Most advertising plays on our lizard brain, on the place within us where we still believe in this conjunction of desirable effects and objects. But if there is something uncanny about the encounter with "secret knowledge" when one thinks about sweat rice, there's something slightly sinister about the realization that such

some way, inadmissible? Among the very few occurrences of the word, perhaps the most famous is in a graffito on a wall in Pompeii. The graffito reads "Peto landicam Fulviae." That is: "I seek Fulvia's clitoris." The graffito was obviously meant to outrage or provoke. But to me, now, it reads almost as if the writer were looking for a lost friend. Or were the words, rather, a cry of dismay?

I was fourteen when I first heard rumours of the clitoris. One of the older boys at Regina Mundi College, the private school I attended in London, Ontario, mentioned the clitoris to me. It was important to know about the clitoris, he said, if you wanted to give a woman pleasure. How the clitoris and pleasure went together wasn't made clear. All I heard was that it existed, and its existence was further bruited by the pornographic writing available at the time. According to rumour, one licked or stroked the "pearl" until the woman was brought to what was, inevitably, the kind of pleasure that rendered her—almost against her will—grateful. So, in a way, the clitoris could be one's ally against its owner. An interesting idea that, as with most ideas encountered in pornography, was not true. The situation was much more complicated. First, if you went right at the clitoris, hunting for it in order to give immediate pleasure and, so, gain immediate gratitude, you got the opposite: a complaint at the irritation. That is, *if* you found it. I mean, nowadays, yes, I have a good idea how things work. But in the beginning, I was anxious that the clitoris would not leave its hood, that I wouldn't be able to coax it out, because I was never quite certain it was "at home." The idea that the clitoris was *the* locus of pleasure for a woman, mixed with my puppy-like desire to please, actually made it a source of anxiety. And, perhaps, the anxiety I used to feel is cognate with the shame Romans felt at the thought of *landica* or with that of the person seeking Fulvia's *landica*. Nowadays when I think of a clitoris, I think of its owner, of course, and of the curious pleasure it gives to run your tongue along the hood of the vulva and to feel the clitoris emerge, on the tip of your tongue, as if a bit of air had coagulated.

basic lizard brain thinking underlies the hundreds of thousands of advertising dollars that go into making Vulva Original seem logical, *un*fantastic, rational. German technology—with its simple lines and rigorous efficiency—isn't at the root of Vulva Original, though that's what Guido Lenssen would have his clients believe. Beneath the campaign for Vulva Original are the caves at Chauvet: wall drawings of "sorcerers," wild animals, and a vulva.

To be clear: As far as I'm concerned, the "sinister" aspect has nothing to do with "magic" or its ritualistic implications. It is, rather, the money and rationalizing that have gone toward trying to make Vulva Original seem more sophisticated than sweat rice. It's as if someone had decided to put the Venus of Willendorf in a business suit.

3. On Touch

I wonder if there's anything more banal than descriptions of how vaginas are to the touch? The words used to describe the feelings are monotonously common: soft, viscous, wet, moist, tight, loose, swollen, puffy, dry, warm. Nor does it get much better when writers try to elaborate. In the land of literature, vaginas feel like silk handkerchiefs, molluscs, a muddy pond bottom, rose petals, warm velvet . . .

Part of the difficulty—for men, anyway—may be that the most overwhelming touch is that of the vagina on the penis. And the penis, having as many nerve endings as the vagina (though not as many as the clitoris), sends a bewildering number of intense signals when it's in the vagina. It's difficult to reduce such a number of impressions to a word or two, difficult to say what the vagina feels like. (It feels soft, viscous, wet, moist . . .)

Once you've experienced the feeling, it is recognizably unique. It becomes a familiar derangement. And reproducing that feel is the basis of an industry, that part of the sex trade taken up with creating artificial vaginas. Now, I don't mean my comments to suggest I feel either scorn for or a moral superiority to those involved in this industry. I feel, rather, curiosity about two aspects of the project.

First, I wonder about the history of artificial vaginas. I suspect we've all heard the faux-Turkish saying "A wife for duty, a boy for pleasure, a melon for ecstasy." I first learned this maxim while reading André Gide and wondered—without wishing to experiment—whether the melon had been refrigerated or not. In the years since then, I've heard other comestibles advanced as suitable: cucumbers, loaves of Wonder bread, liver, oven-warmed butternut squash. In fact, it may be that this impractical use of the larder is what inspired the commercial production of artificial vaginas. Over the years, there have been any number of experiments with plastics, the effort being to find some combination of polymers that will approximate the feeling of a vagina.

Recently, a company called Interactive Life Forms began to manufacture and distribute something called the Fleshlight. According to Wikipedia (and Interactive's patent application):

> The Fleshlight is . . . made of medical and food grade, phthalate-free polymers . . . [T]he insert is not made from latex, plastic or silicone. [The] material is "a company secret covered by a series of US patents" but according to the patent itself (which is public), the material is an elastometric gel being formed from a mixture of 90–94% by weight of plasticizing oil and of 5–9% by weight of a block copolymer comprising an admixture of a styrene ethylene butylene styrene block copolymer and a styrene ethylene propylene styrene block copolymer combined in a ratio of 1:5 to 5:1.

I find it interesting that by experiment we've come to a point where there can be general agreement that an "elastometric gel" is what a vagina feels like. (Enough agreement that Interactive Life Forms has patented its gel.) But the Fleshlight brings up the second thing that sparks my curiosity. The product is so named because the artificial vagina is housed in what looks like a flashlight case. It is wide at the entrance—where the "vaginal" opening has been carved—and long and narrow to accommodate a man's penis. One is, in effect, putting one's penis into a flashlight. I'm not tempted. On the other hand, there is a Japanese item, similar to the Fleshlight but called a "blowfish," in which a "vagina" is housed in what looks like a large fish. I'm even less tempted by the fish, but this is where the ping-pong match between illusion and reality gets heated. If it is all about the *feeling* of the artificial vagina, is it better that the vagina's casing be "realistic" or not? There are makers of artificial vaginas who pride themselves on the realism of their product, providing "vaginal canals" that are not only realistic in feel but also part of *specific* vulvas. You can, if you like, buy an artificial vagina that has been cast from the vulva of, say, Christy Canyon, the porn star.

Naturally, there can be no generalizable answer to the question "Which is better, realistic or unrealistic artificial vaginas?" The world is sexualized—sexually perceived—differently by different men. For some, the Christy Canyon model will be positively arousing. For others, like me, however, the more realistic the "vagina" or torso, the more gruesome the whole thing seems. I can't look at one of the "realistic" models without thinking of axe murderers. And I find the thought of bodies from which the torso or vulva/vagina has been cut completely anerotic.

Why bring all this up, then?

Because it takes us back to John Ruskin and the imagination. I wondered what image Ruskin had of vulvas that he could have found his young bride's private parts so shocking, such a turn-off. Thinking about the "blowfish" or "Christy Canyon model vulva," I feel a revulsion that probably echoes Ruskin's. The intersection of reality, imagination, and desire is so unpredictable that, although I have no doubt the Fleshlight *feels* like a vagina, my mind cannot accept it as vaginal or in any way erotic.

In other words, this is an encounter with the limits of my own imagination. And because I've spent my entire life nurturing my imagination, I'm slightly bewildered to encounter this wall, as

Ruskin himself must have been on his wedding night. The "wall," of course, is another name for the sacred. Or, at any rate, it's an intimation of something beyond the self.

(An aside: Interactive Life Forms also has a Fleshlight inspired by the movie *Avatar*. For this model, the vulva is copper blue without labia, and the opening itself is slightly triangular. It's the corporate interpretation of an "off-world" vulva and, for a moment, the "alien" model brought to my mind the work of Philip José Farmer, stories about forbidden, interspecies love and the transcendence of revulsion. But Interactive Life Form's advertising banished any literary thoughts I had, their motto being: "For centuries man has wondered if he was alone. He has looked to the stars for the answer to one question . . . Is there anything else out there to fuck?" Despite myself, I think there's something almost sublime about this evocation of pathological lust. Our exploration of the universe is brought down to man's desire to put his penis somewhere unfamiliar but soft. For some time after reading that ad, I laughed at the memory of it, but I also began to feel the abyss behind it, the annihilation of worlds by priapic primates. So . . . strange laughter.)

4. On Sound

It's probably impossible to avoid vulgarity when speaking of the sounds a vagina makes, particularly if one wishes to speak about vaginal flatulence.

The phenomenon—the noisy release of air from the vagina during lovemaking—has a rather pleasant name these days: queef. But it's not a common subject of conversation, at least not in the places I usually find myself. It's easy to guess why the subject isn't often mentioned, though. The phenomenon is fleeting, unpredictable, trivial, and of momentary embarrassment, unless you're young. And even then . . .

Also, there's very little to say about queefs. They're surprising when first encountered. They're slightly amusing. One can feel them on one's penis, and the feeling is not unpleasant. And, in my experience, there's nothing noxious about them.

Unlike the other sensual aspects of the vagina, however, queefs can't be exploited for commercial ends. Yes, there are people who delight in the recorded sounds of lovemaking. But of that group, the subset of those aroused by queefs must be too small to support an industry. (Yes, there *is* a website for queef fetishists, but I find it difficult to imagine a "queef nation.") Perverse as it might sound, I think the uselessness of queefs is what makes them worth mentioning. They can't usually be done for a public. They are a thing usually experienced only by those involved. The lovers are usually in the grip of a transport when the thing happens. They occur during moments of absolute intimacy. And though they aren't a signal of that intimacy, they are a dimension of it.

The other sounds a vagina makes—the sound of skin on skin as the penis enters and retreats, the sound of tongue on labia, and so forth—aren't, properly speaking, sounds made by the vagina itself. They're the sounds a vagina makes in concert, and, as sounds, they're both specific and "anonymous."

It's difficult to describe the "sonata for percussion" that takes place during intercourse. That is, it's difficult to describe it without quickly falling into absurdity. I mean, after you've said "wet clapping" or "the rhythmic, open-palmed slapping of a puddle," you quickly get to more obscure and impressionistic versions like "someone a few houses over knocking moist blackboard brushes—or two wet, smallish animals—together." This is the "anonymous" aspect of the sounds made by the penis and vagina: intercourse doesn't particularly sound like intercourse, unless accompanied by the shallow breathing, the moaning, the occasional cries of pleasure that are the things we're attentive to. Once you hear the cries of pleasure, *then* the sounds become so suggestive of lovemaking, the listener can be aroused.

Yes, of course, there is something intimate in the sound of tongue and lips on vulva. It's quiet, barely audible except to the person going down, but it, too, is "anonymous." I remember reading—I wish I remembered where—of a man who could not drink creamy soups because the sound he made while he drank them *inevitably* reminded him of cunnilingus and, so, were an embarrassment.

5. On Vision

I spoke in the introduction about *Playboy* and vulvas and the visual. There's little more for me to say on the subject that hasn't been better said elsewhere by those who've meditated on what used to be called "the male gaze" and its socio-political implications. I know that I am sexually aroused by the *sight* of certain things. But that's a banal matter, and, besides, I'd like to end this essay by talking about a "vulva" that did not arouse me but that remains in memory.

I was in Grade 12 at Regina Mundi College. My cohort had spent four years at Regina Mundi. We all knew each other very well. Just before someone's eighteenth birthday—I can't remember whose—one of my classmates had bought a Valentine's Day edition of *Penthouse* magazine. There wasn't anything unusual about that month's issue, except . . . there was an article devoted to playfully coiffed pubic hair. In honour of St. Valentine, the models had had their pubic hair done by a hairdresser, who had shaped their pubic triangles so that they resembled various things, most notably Valentine's Day hearts. We'd all seen the issue and had been amused.

On the night of the birthday, we'd agreed to meet in the birthday boy's room, where we would drink, eat cake, and hang out after lights out: someone standing guard to look out for the priest on night watch, the rest celebrating. It was a good evening, made definitively memorable by the appearance of two of my roommates in bathrobes. Beneath the bathrobes, they were naked. They had their penises tucked up between their legs and, in honour of the birthday boy, they had shaved their pubic hair into the shape of hearts in imitation of the women we'd seen in *Penthouse*.

It was unexpected, amusing, and, from this distance, curiously ritualistic. There was no sexual component. The unveiling wasn't meant to arouse. As far as I remember, we were, most of us, heterosexual virgins. But there was something to the imitation, an evocation of the vagina for a handful of young men who devoutly desired experience of the real thing. No one would have said we were reverential or awed, but, to some extent, we were, despite the surface irreverence. And the evening reminds me, now that I think of it, of evocations and *in*vocations. There was the fleeting presence of the mysterious, a "mystery" that, despite later experience, retains something of its mystery. (And why not? The young man who felt such instinctive longing for something he'd seen but could not imagine is still alive within me.)

Earlier, I mentioned the cave at Chauvet, in which there's a fascinating mural with depictions of lions, bison, stags, horses, a creature half-man half-bison, and so on. There is also a well-known "Venus." Not a Venus per se, obviously, as the drawings are some thirty thousand years old. But a vulva drawn in charcoal—or black tint—to which a white slit—a vaginal opening—has been added. The Chauvet Venus appears to have been the first thing drawn. Over the years, I've heard theories about the ancient depictions of pudenda. They are evocations of a goddess, they're part of fertility rites, they're graffiti done by irreverent young men . . .

In an article for *The New Yorker* in June 2008, Judith Thurman wrote:

> In the century since the modern study of caves began, specialists from at least half a dozen disciplines—archaeology, ethnology, ethology, genetics, anthropology, and art history—have tried (and competed) to understand the culture that produced them. The experts tend to fall into two camps: those who can't resist advancing a theory about the art, and those who believe there isn't, and never will be, enough evidence to support one.

Not being any kind of expert myself, I have no idea which camp is "right," but my sympathy goes to those who believe there will *never* be certainty about the meaning of prehistoric painting, especially as this pertains to the depictions of vulvas. In evoking the vagina, one is doing many things at once. The vagina, as symbol, can't be reduced to any one thing, whatever the intent of the symbol-maker. (It's a marvellous circumstance, now that I think of it, that the word *vagina* designates a part of the body that is usually invisible, that we need two words (*vulva, vagina*), that one word points to a hiddenness while the other designates a presence.) As with the phallus, evocation ("the calling to mind by naming, citing, or suggesting") and invocation ("the calling on a higher spirit for assistance, support, or inspiration") are inseparable, the sacred and the profane come as one, whatever one might intend.

Though one can accept—when considering cave drawings of the vulva—the intent to invoke a goddess (the sacred) or to call down the spirit of fertility, it's difficult to accept that the artist's personal feelings and experience (the profane) can be entirely put aside. As if to convey this very thing—that is, the personal aspect of the cave drawings—one often finds handprints on the cave walls: a human hand stencilled in black or red so that one sees the outline of the artist's—or *someone's*—hand. A personal mark: simple, striking, and deeply moving.

So, having spent several thousand words evoking the profane and somewhat unintentionally invoking the sacred, there remains one thing for me to do. Hold up my hand, fill a container with powdered charcoal, and splash the tint so that the imprint of my hand is left here, in this place. My name is

André Alexis

I was born in Trinidad, in 1957. My mother's name is Adrina Ena Borde. If, after my death, anyone should wish to reprint this essay, I would be grateful if the date of my death were added, so that my time from my mother's womb to the "great cold" (that other womb) may be known.

Twenty Questions
(Eight, really. It's never as long as you think.)
Merilyn Simonds

I didn't know what to expect. Not a pale, soft snail curled on a taut peach (peach because of the cleft, though it looked more like a rubber ball, it was that exact dull pink, the texture rough).

Want to see? he said and pulled wide the waistband of his shorts.

We were sitting cross-legged, face to face in the white hammock under the guava tree. (White, under that old fruit tree? Wouldn't there have been stains?)

Now show me yours, he said.

But there was nothing to see.

Where did you see your first penis? Your first ear, your first big toe?

I had no brothers, only sisters, who dressed quickly in the dark, or with their backs turned. I never saw my father naked. At night, he wore pyjamas, wine red or navy blue, pale blue in summer. Once, as he was leaving the bathroom, I thought I saw a shadow through the thin cotton. Something moving, close to the skin.

The dog that followed me home from school had a pouch of fur near the back of his belly; now and then something pink slid out, like lipstick from a tube.

For a while I had a horse. I'd climb to the top of the fence and sit splay-legged on the wooden rail watching the stallions, waiting for that gush of urine, the flapping hose between their legs stretching as long as my arm (that's a guess; I never measured).

Later, when I worked in a veterinary clinic, I looked up the words: *sheath, prepuce.*

The story goes, that's how Catherine the Great died. The Russian queen was having sex with a white stallion when the harness suspending the horse over her broke and she was smothered in hot horseflesh.

Could a horse's penis fit inside a woman? Could a dog's? A cat's? Have you tried?

My mother was a nurse. When I was eleven, my mother sat me down at the white table in the white kitchen with a pad of blue airmail paper between us. She drew a pear shape that she called the womb, with antlers rising from the sides, like a Viking helmet. At the tip of each antler, a fat, round pearl.

That's where your eggs are stored, she said. Every month, one is released into the womb. The womb softens and thickens with blood and tissue. That's where the baby grows.

What baby?

She drew an arrow pointing at the mouth of the womb, the part she'd labelled VAGINA.

The baby the father gives you with his sperm.

What if there's no baby?

The womb lets loose the blood and tissue and flushes away the egg. It's called menstruation. The next month, a fresh egg travels down the Fallopian tube into the womb. A new egg every month for the next forty years.

I would bleed and bleed and bleed. Only that arrow, that magic wand, could make it stop.

My mother tapped the paper sharply. You don't want a baby, not for a long time yet.

When is a womb a room, and when is it a tomb? What's a penis got to do with it?

Ah, the magic! I learned to flare my nostrils, crook my eyebrows one at a time, almost got one ear to wiggle, but those tricks were nothing compared to what I found in my boyfriend's pants. A tender snake transformed to a club. A languid finger laid on plush pillow, suddenly a tall boy in a sou'wester.

I felt it first through my clothes, that press like a pencil against my thigh. He moaned; I stifled a laugh. How slender it was, how slight, this thing my mother taught me to fear, this hard wand of life.

Touch it. Please, he said. And I did, sliding my finger down the raw silk skin, tracing the rounded rim of the tip. (My mother drew no boy pictures, wrote no labels. I was in virgin territory here.)

Like this, he said, drawing my fingers around it in a fist.

Hard-on. Boner. Swizzle stick. Shaft. Pole. Rod. Woody. Cock. Pecker. Prick. Wang. Dong. Schlong. Sausage. Mouth organ. Skin flute. This is my rifle, a young soldier chanted, miming, then cupped his crotch and said, this is my gun. It always had a name: Peter, Larry, Willy, Dick. John Thomas. As if it wasn't part of them, more like a friend, separate but close.

They batted up against me, an army coming at me one by one.

I didn't let them in.

Then I did.

Make a list of the penises that have been inside you. Describe each one.

Suddenly, penises were everywhere. You saw them at the movies, barely covered by a sheet; on television, bobbing across football fields; pale shafts dancing at love-ins; something a wife cut off with a carving knife and threw out the car window, into the grass.

Penises were there in the flesh at parties, by the lake, in the pool. I knew where to put my hands, but where to look? Trained in surreptitious glances, I couldn't bring myself to stare head-on. There was a game that couples played: the men stood behind a sheet and pushed their penises through; the women on the other side guessed which belonged to whom. The comfort of sheets.

In a documentary, I saw a foot-long penis. Original equipment, the man said. Other men attached weights to stretch their privates past their knees. They lifted hundred-pound weights with a single erection. One man hooked his penis to a pickup filled with workers and pulled it down the road. Another had to roll it up like a hose to get it into his pants.

I took an interest in science. Among the primates, I learned, human penises are the largest: on average, six inches in length. A horse penis extends a yard. The record length for an elephant penis is six and a half feet, taller than my father. For the blue whale, it's eight. Most birds don't have penises at all. They mate with a "cloacal kiss," a quick brush of nether parts—except for the Argentine lake duck (*Oxyura vittata*), which has a corkscrew penis as long as itself.

Boys liked it when I showed an interest. I told them about the man born with two dicks: he could be hard and soft at the same time, urinate and ejaculate all at once. That's an old joke, they said. He couldn't tell if he was coming or going.

But what about the man who split his penis in half, pierced the tips, and chained them to a gold-link belt around his waist, sometimes to his nipple rings? I saw a picture of that in a book. And a man who had a hard-on for a decade. One injected saline into his scrotum until the skin stretched to a two-foot sac. Another started out as a woman, but had a sheet of flesh sliced from her belly and rolled like a piece of sod to make a penis. When I told them about the music video that showed a man hammering his penis to a piece of wood, the boys yelped and clutched their crotch.

Look how big I am, they'd say. It's all for you. The scientists agreed: take the lake duck, they said. An instance of runaway sexual selection, the preferences of females driving male anatomy to extremes.

I didn't buy it. If I'd met the man with the longest schlong in the world, I would have told him to keep his pants zipped. Once, fed up with being penetrated, I tried to press my own pint-sized erection into the gaping eye of a penis, straining for the active voice.

Mostly, though, I just looked, stealing glimpses at the bulge straining beneath denim or slung in a Speedo bathing suit.

I thought of flowers, fixed to their place, relying on pimping insects to ferry their genes from pistil-penis to anther-womb. No hiding of private parts for them: they waved their pistils like swollen flags above their heads.

Imagine a man with a six-foot penis. What difference would it make?

I never considered that there might be penises that would fail to set off stirrings in that soft spot between my legs. Baby penises, fresh nubbins that demanded to be washed, the sheathing flesh made mobile. New words entered my vocabulary. Smegma. Pearly penile papules. Phimosis. An object of concern, not desire.

But what to make of those baby-carrot erections that poked at the powdered air?

Wizard-boy, I whispered, already practising your tricks.

My own desire remained fierce but focused. One penis, familiar as a breast.

If I had breasts, my husband said, I'd do nothing but play with them all day.

I'd rather play with you, I said, thinking comfort, pleasure, the power to transform from across the room.

The little boys grew. Their penises disappeared from view. Was it that dangling bit of flesh that made them male? Or the blurting noise they made with their lips as they pushed their toy trucks?

I found drawings in the margins of scribblers, noticed my mother's nursing books disturbed, and the art books, too, the same ones I'd paged, looking for proof. When the boys were gone, I repainted their room. On a baseboard in a corner, an odd pencil drawing: two legs and an endless penis that coiled and soared.

What is a boy? What makes him a man?

I love your penis, I said.

It's yours, he said.
Forever?
Even then.

In what other body parts do you share a proprietary interest? A nipple? A clavicle? A knee?

I haven't had an erection since I was fifty-seven, my uncle said.

I leaned over the bed, slipped the peebottle out from between his legs. His pubic hair was black and thick. His eighty-four-year-old penis didn't look a day over twenty. I dabbed a tissue at the tip.

Comfortable? I said, but he was deep in his morphine dream. I sat waiting for him to die, thinking of pictures I'd seen of dead men, old men sprawled in stone doorways or across dusty dirt roads, clothes in shreds, penises exposed. How ordinary those dead members looked, no different from a thumb or a nose, only a little less life-worn. Time leaves its tracks on skin bared to the air, but a penis passes the years under cover, rarely sees the light of day.

Breasts sag, vaginas droop and dry, but a penis never shows its age.

If this is the answer, what is the question?

My Womb Works

Heather Kuttai

I remember the first time I saw my womb. It was on my birthday, October 7, 1996, and as I peered into the ultrasound screen I saw a grainy, black-and-white, amorphous shape that was the "home" for my unborn baby. The technician showed us our baby's arms, legs, and beating heart. I was keenly aware of my own rapid heartbeat and how I had to remind myself to breathe. My husband, Darrell, and I could hardly believe what we were seeing. There was really a baby in there. A baby growing in *my* womb.

The womb, of course, is the organ in a female mammal where a fetus develops. But the womb is more than that: it is a body part distinctive to women, a thing that only we have. And possessing a functional womb that has allowed me to grow my babies (I now have a fourteen-year-old boy and a five-year-old girl) is especially meaningful to me, since I am a paraplegic who uses a wheelchair.

As a six-year-old girl who survived a motor-vehicle accident that resulted in a spinal cord injury, I lived with a decidedly different set of developmental, social, and biological expectations than non-disabled girls my age experienced as they grew up. It was assumed that I would always need someone to look after me; that I would not be able to live independently; that I would not be able to attract a man, date, marry, and certainly not have a sexual relationship, have children, or be able to look after those children. Because my spinal cord was injured in my early childhood, I believe this expectation that I would live a socially and sexually barren life was even more poignant for me than for women who acquire their disabilities later in life; I faced a barren life with a barren womb. Why would I need a uterus anyway?

This typical asexual status often attributed to people with disabilities was, I believe, stronger for me than for other people who are injured after they have achieved their sexual identities, because, unlike people who experience spinal cord injuries later in life, I had no opportunity to develop an "adult" construction of sexuality or the prepubescent or adolescent constructions of sexuality. After a spinal cord injury, sexual identities and adult social roles are often denied. At age six, I had not yet, of course, developed sexually in physical, social, or emotional ways. I was just simply too young.

It is incredibly difficult to live without that sexual identity. I remember particularly struggling once I entered adolescence while living in a rural farm community in Saskatchewan. I wanted to believe I was a "real" girl who was turning into a "real" woman, and I wanted others to believe it too. While in Grade 7, my English teacher assigned our class the task of writing an essay on our favourite song lyrics. All of the girls chose a song from the top of the *Billboard* chart that was constantly played on the radio, but I chose a song that was not as popular among my preteen classmates. Heavily influenced by my sister-in-law's Beatles obsession, I chose "Woman" by John Lennon. I chose it because it is a beautiful song and easy to sing to, but also because the lyrics fascinated me. Lennon was, of course, singing to Yoko Ono, but I was less concerned with their connection and more intrigued with how strong and powerful he believed her to be. Perhaps it was this song that lit a spark for the interest I would later take in feminism, because Lennon begins the song by whispering "for the other half of the sky . . ." a statement of his respect for women. In the liner notes of the CD that commemorates what would have been Lennon's seventieth birthday, Anthony DeCurtis writes that Lennon wrote it not only for Yoko Ono, but for all women. The lyrics for "Woman" hinted that women were strong and influential and that men could be vulnerable and need help. That was the first time I'd heard that kind of message.

The song triggered questions: What did it mean to be a woman? Would I ever be seen as a woman? Was I capable of being a woman? And when on earth was I ever going to get my period? As I remember it, a lot of girls my age felt the same way about their first period. I was twelve years old and in Grade 6 when I first read Judy Blume's coming of age novel *Are You There God? It's Me, Margaret*, about a group of girls who were preoccupied with developing breasts, first bras, and first periods. As I remember it, the book was so popular during this time that the school library could not keep it on the shelf. It circulated among the girls in my class. We were all curious, anxious to read it and to understand this silenced secret. Like Margaret, the main character, I was desperate to get my period. Any way that one chooses to look at it, menstruation is the most striking biological indicator of being a woman, and I was obsessed with the idea that if I could just get my period, it would mean that my body was like everyone else's, that I, too, could be a "real" girl who was becoming a "real" woman.

Now that I am an adult, I am glad I do not have to relive those years of adolescent angst, but I still sometimes question my femininity, my womanhood. Even now, with two children and a partner who has loved me for more than twenty years, I still feel a twinge of displacement when I enter a lingerie store or ask my hairdresser to make my hair look pretty. I take some comfort in knowing I am not the only one who feels this way. I had the good fortune to recently give a reading on my book *Maternity Rolls* to a group of women who use wheelchairs. They all disclosed their struggles with their real or perceived notions of femininity and their choice to have children or not. Many talked about how complicated their new bodies were when it came to lovemaking. One woman with a spinal cord injury similar to mine, who was injured just a few years before me, disclosed to us that her parents chose to "sterilize" her when they learned she would never walk again.

Her story stuck with me. Because while some women cannot use their wombs to have children and some women choose not to become mothers, my new friend's ability to choose what she did with her womb was taken from her. She told me that it took time but that she has found peace with what was done, has a wonderful extended family, and does not need children of her own to fulfill her life. However, she also admitted that sometimes she wonders what mothering would have been like.

I, on the other hand, was fortunate enough to be able to very clearly and consciously choose to have children. I was well into my twenties before I began to imagine this role for myself, and I remember being preoccupied with the idea of wanting to know what the kind of love between a mother and a child was like. And as a surprising twist to the decision to have a child, while I was pregnant, I started to feel whole and complete. For the first time, I found the female identity I had been searching for. I wore my round belly like a badge of honour, as though I could now prove that I was a card-carrying member of the club called "Woman." It was not that my pregnancies made me feel special, but rather that my pregnancies made me feel more "normal" than I ever had before.

The feminist voice in my head tells me that I should not have needed to become pregnant to feel like a so-called normal woman. In her book *The Politics of Reproduction*, Mary O'Brien argues that when we question the causes of women's suppression, the answers tend to point to our reproductive functions. Furthermore, feminist and social activist bell hooks argues in her 1990 essay "Homeplace: A Site of Resistance" that by

> romanticizing motherhood, employing the same terminology that is used by sexists that women are inherently life-affirming nurturers, feminist activists reinforce central tenets of male supremacist ideology. They imply that motherhood is a woman's truest vocation; that women who do not mother, whose lives may be focused more exclusively on a career, creative

work, or political work, are missing out, are doomed to live emotionally unfulfilled lives.

Having felt excluded from embodiment, feminist, and sociological literature so often, I struggled with writing this essay because I did not want to exclude the experiences of women who do not use their wombs to have children. I wrote with the constant awareness that while I connect with my womb for the reproductive abilities that it had/has, I also know that not all women are able to have the experience of growing a baby in their womb, that not all women choose to use their womb for growing babies, and that wombs can be a source of pain and illness.

In writing about my pregnancy and childbirth experiences, I did not want to contribute to the patriarchal notion that assumes all women are born to be mothers. I know this, I studied this, I believe this. My choice to have children, to use my body and my womb to grow them and bring them into the world, should not make me feel more female, or more like a woman, but it does. It does. Of course it does. Because as bell hooks says in the beginning of that same paragraph, "women who choose to bear children need no longer to fear that this choice excludes them from recognition by the feminist movement." This assertion reminds me of what Alice Walker, another writer I admire, says: that the basic principle of feminism is the right to choose.

Perhaps I was lucky that I did not have to live with the ubiquitous cultural belief that I would someday "have to" have children. In as much as I grew up without a female sexual identity, I was also freed from the overwhelming assumption that I would necessarily have to live out my life in a particular way. I found tremendous personal power when I chose to have children, and that surprised me. I was also surprised to hear how much power my womb had. When I was concerned that my spinal cord injury would impair my ability to push during the birth of my son, my doctor reassured me: "Don't worry. Your uterus knows what to do. I will be there to help, and I will coach you on what to do, but your womb will do all the hard work."

I wanted to believe him, but everything I had researched and read about a woman with a spinal cord injury giving birth led me to believe I would not be able to push, and therefore how the delivery would go was a bit of a mystery. When Darrell and I decided to go to the hospital late one night because I thought I had a bladder infection, my doctor examined me and laughingly told me I was having eight-centimetre dilated bladder spasms. This was labour, as I knew it.

As I lay on the delivery table, Dr. T. asked me if I wanted to try to push. I told him I did not know how and that I had not been taught. Darrell and I thought there was no point in learning how to push if I was not capable of it. But Dr. T. believed I should try. He gave a brief tutorial, encouraged me to visualize, and when the next contraction came, I did it. I pushed!

As Darrell held my legs and braced my back, I gripped the sides of the table, and using all my upper body strength, I bore down and sweated like I imagine every woman, disabled or not, does. After about forty-five minutes, Dr. T. encouraged me to reach down and touch my son's head. The next thing I knew, our baby was born. I was overwhelmed by his miraculous birth, but I was also equally astonished at the capability of my body, my womb.

My womb works. It is a powerful and beautiful organ that brought life into the world. It occupies the very centre of me. It helped to heal a broken girl who was desperately searching for her purpose and identity. It is true that my womb gave life to my children, but it also gave a new life to me, the chance to be reborn into a new sense of self.

Life with My Girls

Lynne Van Luven

I have everything I had twenty years ago, only it's all a little lower.

—Gypsy Rose Lee, dancer, writer, and agente provocateuse

"Just stand still, let me measure you." My mother ran her frayed cloth measuring tape around the middle of my chest, right where the tender points had started to sprout. "Now breathe naturally."

Two weeks later, the brown-paper package from the Eaton's catalogue centre in Winnipeg arrived at the post office, addressed to Box 166, Dysart, Saskatchewan, and my dad brought it home from town with the rest of the mail. Like many farm families of the late 1950s, we ordered most of our clothes from the catalogue. But I wouldn't be showing off this purchase the way I did new shoes or a sweater. You couldn't really call it . . . clothing. And I certainly didn't want my pesky brother, Raymond, four years younger, to know what was going on. Even though the small, soft rectangle seemed to glow red from the corner of the kitchen cupboard, I ignored it until after supper.

"Come on upstairs," said Mom. "Let's see how these fit."

Inside the package were two cheap white cotton bras (Charmode, two for $3.95) with narrow elastic straps and a row of three hooks and eyes that fastened at the centre of the back. Top-stitched in concentric circles, the cups culminated in sharp points. Grumpily self-conscious, I tried one on. I felt strung up, harnessed more tightly than Paint, my pinto pony. The pointy tips collapsed inwards on my chest, sort of like deflated volleyballs, only conical.

My mother patted me briskly on the shoulder. "You'll grow into them."

Not if I can help it, I thought. I'd already tried sleeping on my stomach to squash my growths. I'd also attempted plastering bands of adhesive tape over my chest to starve the buds of air so they would fall off, the way warts eventually did after you suffocated them with Band-Aids. Or maybe if I took a few loops of that black electrical tape out of my dad's garage . . .

When I lay awake in bed that night stewing about my breasts, I folded my hands flat over them and pressed down, hard. The way I saw it, their uninvited presence thrust me directly into the ranks of the animals on the farm, the ones with udders and teats—the cows and the sows—all of whom were relegated to two stark roles in life: producing food or becoming it. Sometimes they did both, one right after the other. Even mother cats, as they lay on their sides to let their kittens suckle, signalled abject passivity to me. First they screamed horribly when the tomcats jumped them; then they pumped out half a dozen kittens of varying hues and patterns; finally, the nursing kittens rampaged all over them. And their milk was never enough: they also had to hunt rapaciously, dragging birds and mice and rats back to the barn to feed their progeny.

Breastlike appendages, as far as I could see, brought nothing but trouble: when we milked the cows, we tied them up and yanked on their TITS, which sounded nothing like TEATS; we pulled and squeezed until long streams of milk squirted into the empty galvanized pails. And, as far as I could observe, men eyed women with the same judgmental eye they reserved for prime heifers and breed sows. And now, as a result of these mutant mounds on my chest, I was being forced into their bovine and porcine ranks.

In his book *Carnal Knowledge: A Navel Gazer's Dictionary of Anatomy, Etymology, and Trivia*, Charles Hodgson tells us that "like a number of other basic body words in English, *breast* is as old as the language itself." Versions of the word appeared as *breasto* in such Latin manuscripts as the illustrated *Lindisfarne Gospels* around the year 700. He notes that the word *breast* was found translated into Old English bibles as early as the year 1000. Even had I, as an agonized eleven-year-old, known about the breast's impressive etymology, it would not have comforted me. I wasn't into language and theory then. At least thirty years would pass before I'd learn about the Neolithic settlement of Çatalhöyük in southern Anatolia, where, from 7500 to 5700 BCE, breasts were revered as instruments of motherhood until patriarchy turned them into erotic symbols.

I know, of course, that the way I am remembering my early "breastory" is somewhat skewed, but I had been naively happy in my Pre-Brassiere (PB) era. Wearing my little white cotton undershirts, I galloped about, innocently invisible, just another kid. But the advent of puberty, followed by node growth, resulted in AB (After Brassiere), and for the rest of my life I would be enslaved by that "woman's supportive undergarment" invented in 1913 by Mary Phelps Jacob (later known as Caresse Crosby), to supplant chemises, corsets, and bandiers.

Paul Rutherford, in his pre–*Mad Men* book *A World Made Sexy: Freud to Madonna*, recounts the famous "I dreamed" advertising campaign run by Maidenform from 1949 to 1969 to promote its brassieres. The first such ad ("I dreamed I went shopping in my Maidenform Bra") quickly morphed into more adventurous settings ("I dreamed I went on a safari in my Maidenform Bra") in the one hundred subsequent ads. Soon ("I dreamed I was a toreador in my Maidenform Bra"), the black-and-white ads were supplanted by colour. The campaign's legacy was huge, as Rutherford notes:

> Crucial to each ad was the display of a young woman,
> supposedly caught up in a dream, who exposed her
> bra-encased breast and much of her upper body, in

some social place to an unseen audience. Underwear became outerwear. The private was now the public.

Toward the end of their twenty-year run, Maidenform ads even breached the august confines of *The New Yorker*. Although I was resistant to the Maidenform message of joyous freedom, I still recall the taglines, as do many women my age.

My reality did not mimic the Maidenform myth: even worse than the elastic straps across my chest and shoulders was the immediate result when I wore my new harness to school: suddenly, I had to endure snickers and unabashed stares from all the "big boys" (those older than the norm) in Grades 7 and 8. And then the ensuing bra-strap snapping by Donald, the mouth-breathing boy who sat behind me. I thought he was as unappealing as a poplar fence picket, but he dared to strap-snap me, revelling in his power to elicit the other boys' guffaws. I hated how something *he* did to *me* made me feel smaller, made the other boys laugh *at* me. Decades later, I would better understand my mortification when I discovered what feminists theorized as "the male gaze," the glances that made women the object of someone else's attention rather than the subject and prime actor in their own lives.

Thank Hera, no one has wanted (or dared) to bra-snap me in decades, but when I think about breasts, I feel confounded by the contradictions surrounding them. I do cherish the occasional golden memory: a stolen afternoon, the futon suffused with late-day sunlight, the gentle man beside me caressing me tenderly, telling me how "beautiful" were my breasts. He and I should never have been in bed together, and the affair was briefer than brief, but he did seem to genuinely understand the female body, and in those moments I did feel glad to have breasts.

So, yes, I am mired in my memories, as well as my own culture and demographic. I regularly remind myself that there may still be the occasional place on earth where Barbie dolls and Pamela Anderson's best features are unknown, places absent of air-brushed versions of women who are overtly full on their torsos and incredibly skinny on their bottom halves, women prone to tipping forward on their stilettos. In her excellent 1997 book *A History of the Breast*, Marilyn Yalom observes that the meaning of the breast changes according to times and countries. "Both Northern and Southern Europe inherited a Greco-Roman tradition," she writes,

> but one might say that Aphrodite has reigned in Italy and France, whereas Athena has prevailed in England and Germany . . . Although one must always be wary of national generalizations, it is safe to say that the Catholic Mediterranean has historically been more indulgent toward public delight in the bosom than the Protestant countries of Northern Europe and America.

Is that observation true any longer, I wonder, colonized as North American imagination is by the parade of *Playboy* Bunnies, breast-augmented starlets, and endless porn websites focused on big boobs?

Consider how young female singers in all genres (even opera: look at the plaudits heaped on singer Measha Brueggergosman when she shed dozens of pounds and became more slinky) of the music industry are expected to flaunt their bodies. American singer Janet Jackson's "wardrobe malfunction" generated a ludicrous furor following the 2004 Super Bowl: aghast Middle Americans, ridiculous headlines about "Nipplegate," a legal tussle over fines levied upon CBS by the US Federal Communications Commission. But popular culture's maw requires ever-greater non-virgin sacrifices. And in the wake of Madonna's early tutelage, Lady Gaga and Rihanna have proven that lithe, pragmatic young singers today view their bodies as "booty," which they are happy to self-pirate in order to gain celebrity and advance their careers. Their presence in twenty-first-century popular culture induces non-celebrity young women to flaunt their own bosoms, bellies, and butts with casual impunity. These days, plunging necklines are ubiquitous in work-places and classrooms; "boob jobs" seem to be booked as casually as my generation schedules dental hygiene. So, yes, I'm a woman whose dissonance about her own breasts is a sadly dated emotion. Nevertheless, I agree with feminist film critic Molly Haskell when she claims that "the mammary fixation is the most infantile, and the most American, of the sex fetishes."

And still . . . while one segment of society adores a flaunted breast, yet another recoils in horror as we muddle pruri-ence and commercial rapacity while feigning shock. Even as stodgy an institution as the Bay has joined the surge: "New & Exclusively Ours . . ." reads a midsummer flyer thrust into my local newspaper. "Poof, it's Magic! Maidenform's 'Like Magic' bra increases your bust by TWO sizes. Only $24.99. Sizes 32A to 36C." And so a new version of the Maidenform campaign is thrust at us.

It's perversely ironic that, in North America, in what neo-conservatives like to call a post-feminist era, breasts are still polarized as objects of either seduction or shame. Why haven't we all (myself included) evolved beyond these primal emotions about breasts? Why, for instance, does a woman still fear a reprimand from the police if she goes topless on a hot day while males can flaunt the most gross beer bellies imaginable? Why, in magazines, movies, and everyday male behaviour, does the breast continue to be the most attention-grabbing aspect of female anatomy? And why are women still susceptible to such delineations of their bodies? In this age of confession and celebrity, female mammaries attract even more notice than butts and hips. Why else would a quarter-million American women spend between six thousand and twelve thousand dollars (some of them using credit to finance their new boobs for one hundred and five dollars a month) to obtain "breast enhancement surgery"? (The average cost for saline breast implants in Canada is $6,572—not covered by medical insurance, though breast reductions are if size affects a patient's physical or mental well-being.) It seems to me that humans' conflicting feelings about breasts begin with size and function and unravel into fears of temptation and damnation, as well as arcane fetishes and fantasies.

Despite the overwhelming burgeoning of porn websites—which, one would think, would induce a certain blasé (if not plain bored) response to the naked human form—North American society is still at odds with itself when it comes to breast functionality. A 2003 survey for the US Centers for Disease Control and Prevention found that 30 per cent of 3,976 respondents were not "comfortable" with mothers nursing in public, even though the act is not illegal. Every few months, some breastfeeding mother somewhere in North America offends someone who objects to the "public nudity" of the act. For instance, in 2008, Calgary-based WestJet airlines caused a controversy when one of its flight attendants asked a nursing mother to cover up with a blanket while she breastfed her child; apparently, her maternal act made other passengers feel "uncomfortable." One can only conclude that such objections spring from people who see breasts only as sex organs. Don't they know that breast milk itself has antibacterial and healing properties, that it can be used to soothe an eye infection, to heal skin abrasions and wounds, even to stop mosquito bites from itching? Why isn't it bottled and sold as a natural cure? The ultimate home-based business!

Perhaps because of their hard work as nourishers of newborns, breasts have not been misappropriated the way female genitalia have: what can be more insulting than one man calling another a cunt? On the other hand, there is nothing positive about announcing that something (or someone) has gone "tits up." And the word *titillation* still elicits snickers from little boys. I doubt I will live long enough to compile a complete list of all the slang terms for women's breasts. Consider these few gleanings:

From Yiddish slang: kishkas; Tsitskehs; from cockney rhyming slang: Georgie Bests; from younger colleagues: sweater muffins, sweater puppets, The Girls, kittens; from a lesbian graduate student's survey of her online contacts: glory shelf, tatties, the pointer sisters, sallys, breasticles, tots, tic tacs, yummer muffins. Terms overheard in bar rooms: tits, knockers, hooters, lungs, jugs, yayas; harvested from numerous and lengthy Internet lists: Jane Russells, melons, baps, bubs, ta-tas, bubbies, bristols; adapted from Aussie slang: norxs, wazoos, bazooms, bajungas, gazongas.

Even academics chime in: a Zimbabwean English professor observes that his native Shona language differentiates between mangos, for "sharp pointed young ones," and *matende*, the same word as jugs, "except in this case the sense is of pumpkins, hence large ones." "In Mohawk," reports one of my university colleagues, "we say *Noondas* (just the way it sounds). And *Ononda'* (oh-Noondahs) is a word that means hills and milk and boobs in our language."

Such variety, such a cornucopia of phrases. (Come to think of it, isn't the cornucopia sort of breast-shaped?) Still, my closeted puritan self is relieved that a few people still practise reserve when it comes to the poor old breast. "We didn't go around *talking* about them," a retired Englishman protests, aghast, when I inquire about public-school terms for breasts.

"We never mentioned them," his wife adds. "Well, once in a while we may have said 'full chested' or 'well endowed.'"

Yes, we did. I have always treasured actress Jane Russell's 1970s commercials for the Playtex Cross Your Heart bra, in which she confides her concerns to "full-figured gals." (Thanks to the exploitation of Howard Hughes, Jane had weathered a lot of ogling by the time she made those commercials: her jutting breasts (38D) first attained fame in the 1943 movie *The Outlaw*.) We need special "support," after all, we full-figured gals. And in this anorexic era of the gamine, the waif, the twig actress, the stylish androgynous chest for women and "heroin chic," we full-figured gals probably need moral support most of all. Because, frankly, don't big boobs seem terribly déclassé?

Breasts begin developing in the human embryo about two weeks after conception. By the final eight weeks of pregnancy, female hormones cause breast cells to secrete the liquid substance known as colostrum, sometimes called "witches' brew." In both male and female newborns, swellings beneath the nipples and aureolae can be felt. I find it sublimely reassuring to remember that, from infancy to just before puberty, there is no difference between the male and female breasts. Only when the tsunami called puberty sweeps over the female body is estrogen released to begin the burgeoning process. Mature female breasts consist of four structures: lobules or glands, milk ducts, fat, and connective tissue. When you think of them that way, all the fussing, the trussing, the ogling, and the whistling seem rather silly. As Julia Roberts's character asks in the film *Notting Hill*, "Breasts—how can you be so interested in them? . . . Every second person in the world has got them . . ."

It seems only fair to admit that some men may just never *get* the previous sentence. One of my male readers reminded me that "breasts are one of the most obvious ways in which men and women differ," so it is natural to differentiate between large- and small-breasted women. "We have," he admonishes me, "a deeply complicated relationship to others' bodies." Okay, I concede that. But—call me intractable—I would rather be seen as the sum of my parts than for two particular bits.

Of course, not every woman has breasts these days: I recently spent an evening regaling a houseguest, a friend's new partner, with my research on breast slang only to discover that she'd had a double mastectomy to treat breast cancer several years ago. I should have thought of that, since the most common cancer among Canadian women is breast cancer. According to the Canadian Cancer Society, 11 per cent of Canadian women are expected to develop breast cancer in their lifetime. In 2009, more than twenty-two thousand women were diagnosed with it. Of those women found to have breast cancer, fifty-four hundred will die. Yes, our yummer muffins, our kittens, our bazooms, our girls, are lethal entities: they can kill us.

I can't decide which is worse: being young with breasts or being old with them. Consider young first: most of my memories of high school dating are marred by images of sweaty back- or front-seat tussles when boys tried to (a) weasel a hand under my bra and/or (b) fumble fruitlessly to undo its hooks. Breasts, it seems, are like mountains: man feels they must be conquered because they are there. And somehow, my having them gave others the right to invade my private space. Shy, ashamed, no longer invisible, I cringed every time some yobbo on the street hollered, "Nice tits," his coarse equivalent of "Hubba hubba!" I was in my mid-thirties, a feminist, when a total stranger in Heraclion, Crete, whipped out his arm and copped a hard grab-and-twist as I walked past. Too shocked to retort or act, I simply wobbled on my way.

"Since the nineteenth century," Marilyn Yalom says, "the demands on the breast have multiplied with the speed of everything else in an industrial and post-industrial age." I'd like to report that my own development proceeded happily apace once the initial hell of puberty abated, but that would be a lie. As I matured, I went through my plump phase (one that has merrily returned with menopause, I should confess). My breasts fluffed up even more, and so did my hips. By the time I was sixteen, when everyone was supposed to be a skinny hippie, I looked downright matronly. I took to sewing my own clothes, with deep bust darts, to accommodate my bosom. How bitterly I envied my friend Janie, who remained "flat as a board." And when I looked at my mother's cushiony chest, I knew my future was pneumatic. (At least until old age flattened my "assets.")

I hadn't read enough back then to know how lucky a mammal I actually was. At least, being a normal primate, I had only two breasts. But nature loves variety, as I was reminded when I bent over to milk Betty and Daisy, cows that sashay around with four teats and are not too particular about their grooming. But consider the poor Virginia opossum, cursed with thirteen mammary glands. Imagine trying to find a bra to stable that odd number of nipples. Even the prosaic farm sow has sixteen mammaries, all the better to appease her squealing offspring.

"Just take a right at the corner there and follow the pink line," the young woman at the reception desk instructs me. And I walk myself along the Victoria General Hospital corridor to have my biennial breast mashing.

Getting a mammogram has never been my—or anyone else's—favourite activity, even though we aging women are urged to include it in our regular health-care maintenance, along with feeling ourselves up frequently to ensure none of those nasty little growths have invaded our Girls. But I have yet to meet one woman, large- or small-breasted, who likes slapping her boobies on that cool metal shelf to be X-rayed. (Mind you, it's far less uncomfortable than the dreaded "internal exam," where you lie helpless, legs asplay, as the cold speculum invades your inner sanctum.)

"Any concerns with your breasts?" the technician asks once I've taken off the paper gown worn from change cubicle to mammogram room.

"Only the droop factor," I crack, hoping she's not looking at my muffin top.

"Tell me about it," she jokes, even though she's twenty years younger than I am and slim as a wand.

When I'm dieting, I always resent my breasts: they add weight. "Lose ten ugly pounds: cut off your head," we used to taunt each other as teens. Breasts are not nearly that heavy: medium-sized women estimate that their breasts weigh about five pounds apiece. Wrong. One average-sized female breast weighs a pound. And it will shrink if you diet.

"Move your shoulder. Reach up. Arch your arm. Now, hooold your breath," the attendant repeats as she positions my naked right breast over the cool metal surface. Once again the upper plate descends, my flesh is compressed and a *sszzzz* sounds as the breast is filmed.

Yes, growing old with breasts means that you worry about more serious things than the occasional masher. When radiologists study the exams, they look for cysts, calcifications, and any other abnormalities. And now there's some debate about how effective mammograms really are, especially for large-breasted women, but health-care professionals still recommend them—and health insurance still covers them. About two weeks after my stroll down the pink path at VGH, I got a letter from the BC Cancer Agency's Screening Mammography Program that informed me my pair were "normal" and reminded me to get a Pap smear (result of Dr. Georgios Papanikolaou's research back in 1928) every two years.

Okay, all right: life with breasts hasn't all been tough noogies. I have had a satisfying life; a few nice men have enjoyed stroking and kissing them, while I have reciprocated with my own frissons. Mostly, My Girls have probably been more appreciated by others than by me. On the other hand, since I am childless, my lay-about breasts have remained relentlessly unfunctional while slowly slipping in their decorative capacity. Unused for nursing, they have had a darn easy life—no cracked nipples, no surge and shrink, few stretch marks. "Have you ever considered the value of attrition?" I sometimes ask The Girls when we shower. "Planned obsolescence? Just downsizing naturally?" They proffer only silent stoicism.

Even though life after fifty renders most women invisible to street maulers, our breasts hang on, tenacious if not perky. Aside from the fact that nobody lunges to ogle or fondle them anymore, gravity gets them down. During my first job as a small-town reporter, I was aghast when the only female columnist at the *Red Deer Advocate* reported a sure-fire way to tell if your breasts could be called perky: if you could hold a pencil in the fold that formed where your breast cleaves to your chest, your boobs definitely had left the Land of Perk. And that's Not Good. That's why so many women spend valuable time and money ensuring that their breasts are well supported; to fail in this area connotes a lack of self-respect; we either buy shockingly expensive "undergarments" or give over to Da Droop. "I cannot possibly retire yet," one of my friends lamented recently. "I need to buy new bras this year."

"Well," I said to my husband on a sultry July morning, "Since I am here, I might as well check it out. Who knows when we'll be back this way again?"

"It" was Lily's Lingerie Limited, a steadfast Halifax business for three decades. Lover of alliteration that I am, how could I pass it up? "Sexy, elegant, intimate," purr the store's online ads. "Bra-Fitting Experts, European styling, 30 years of experience." Furthermore, *Chatelaine* magazine has dubbed the shop one of the Top Ten in Canada.

Duly enticed, I tripped down Spring Garden Road to Dresden Row, climbed up the tiled steps—and felt my eyeballs sproing from my head. Never in all my years had I seen so many different colours of bras: brandy, burgundy, chartreuse, champagne, fuchsia, flame, puce, purple, sienna, silver. Most of them were lacy, and few of them utilitarian. Far too bordello-like for me, I thought as I stood gobsmacked in the middle of the floor as a slender reed of a girl approached.

When I blurted out my need for a fitting, she waved over another sylph. "Kelly will assist you," she said. Once behind the dressing room curtain, I was grilled and measured by the triple-A apparition. Had I been fitted for a bra before? What kind of a bra did I like? What fabric? What design and colour?

"I just want something to support The Girls," I said, gesturing to my poitrine.

Kelly frowned. "Hmmm, we may not have many selections in your size."

Twenty-five sweaty minutes later, after stripping and stretching and strapping The Girls back in, I tottered to the till clutching a black, seamlessly supportive structure, on sale for one hundred and twenty-five dollars. The cashier tenderly shrouded my purchase in hot-pink tissue paper.

"Biggest mistake all women make?" she asked me. "Wearing the wrong-sized bra. Almost always too small."

Well, I certainly could not be accused of *that*: Kelly had fitted me with a size 36F. Who knew cups galumphed that far into the alphabet?

That evening, 36F and I sashayed out to dinner with my husband. By the end of the evening, despite fine sushi and a lovely stroll, The Girls were carping: they felt too restricted, and consequently out of sorts. (Absent my one hundred and twenty-five dollars, so did I.) Back to Lily's we all traipsed early the next morning. This time, after I'd ensured I could return yesterday's bra, another young woman measured me. She was, I rejoiced to see, a little chubby and more sympathetic to The Girls and me. She snapped a couple of samples on and off us before finding one that sat better on my rib cage. Alas, at $229, my lacy new caramel-coloured Melody Seamless Bra was not on sale. I would not be back again. But The Girls were happy.

But enough breast-beating: by now it's clear that I have always regarded mine as excess baggage: spongy nuisances that began growing without my permission, required a lot of maintenance, and turned into tenacious appurtenances that I have hauled around for a lifetime. They are a drag during exercise and cause lumpen deformation of fine tailoring. Nevertheless, I am thankful they have not yet killed me. I have never hated them enough to fork out thousands for breast-reduction surgery nor felt compelled to have them removed as part of a sex change. So, perhaps, after all these decades, it is time to make peace with The Girls, to stop thinking of Them as "out there" and finally incorporate Them fully into my sense of self: Mine, My Girls, for better or for worse.

My Flat Cree Ass

Candace Fertile

So I go to the hold shelf at my local library to pick up the book I've ordered. It's not there. I hand over my library card. The librarian calls up my info and turns to me, suddenly blushing. "Oh," she says, "it should be there. I'll go check." She can't say the title. Neither can I, for some reason. I reorder *Embracing Your Big Fat Ass*. I tell the librarian, who is looking at me in a peculiar way, that I need the book for research. I back away slowly, wondering who would take someone else's book. Especially this one. The book thief must be in the library because the computer system prevents people from checking out a book on hold. I ponder, slinking about to see if I can spot my book, but realize that even if I do, I am unlikely to find the words to retrieve it from the person who wants it more than I do.

Bootylicious: voluptuous, especially the derrière, and causing sexual salivation. Not a word that could ever be applied to me. In fact, given my genetic stew, I used to think (when I thought about it at all) that having a flat ass was normal—it certainly was for all the women in my family—my grandmother (from whom the Cree flows), my eight aunts, my mother, and my numerous cousins.

The gluteus maximus (ass, backside, butt, bum, buttocks, buns, can, rear end, derrière, seat, backside, fanny, keister, hindquarters, haunches, rump, tush, heinie, tail, cheeks, moon) is the largest muscle in the body. But as anyone with a boney butt will attest, muscle is not comfy to sit on. A little padding helps. Maybe that's why so many cultures practise crouching with the butt airborne rather than flattened on the ground. Hmm, I expect there's a study on this right now, but I have a deadline for this essay, which I've already missed twice—a situation that really means I have failed to slap my flat ass into my office chair and sit in front of my computer for hours to ponder the wonderful possibilities of butt fat. I have no time (or really any inclination) to research methods of sitting. I'd rather be lying down.

The Venus of Willendorf, a statue carved between 24,000 and 22,000 BCE, depicts a woman with large breasts, hips, and ass. Its meaning is not known, but since fertility is crucial to the continuation of the human race, it may be that the exaggerated features are celebrating the female power of childbearing and ability to survive the harsh, cold climate of northwestern Europe at the time. Who knows? At different points in time, curvaceous women have been idolized. I contrast the image of the buxom, broad-hipped, large-assed woman with the extremely thin models in a recent *Vogue* magazine. Although fashion models do not have flat asses, they do tend to have a particular body type, whether genetically ordained or food-deprived. Robert Altman's 1994 movie *Prêt-à-Porter* features a stunning conclusion when the runway models come out—all nude. They look like walking wire hangers, presumably Altman's message. Very thin women still need to have breasts, hips, and a backside to be considered sexy. Think of Barbie, with her impossibly tiny waist, gravity-defying breasts, and pert butt.

Size was never an issue until I got to high school. I never thought about my body much—my only concern was that the various parts worked. I did experience moments of grief in junior high when I grew seven inches in one year, going from being the regular size of a girl my age (five feet, two inches) to being the second-tallest kid in the class, including the boys. And I think my feet were bigger than Tall Guy's. Both of my parents were above average in height, and I had expected that five-foot-two would not last. Those seven inches did make me rather formidable on the basketball court. And so did my feet—my mother's explanation, which captured me with a weird logic, posited that if I had smaller feet, I would tip over.

But butts? Breasts were a much bigger deal for girls, and no matter the size of the mammaries, no girl I knew was happy with her frontage. Too much, too little, too unbalanced, too noticeable in any case. If we could have sat on our boobs, we probably would have. But most of the time we were sitting on our butts, in tidy rows, and in tidy skirts or dresses even if it was forty below because back then girls couldn't wear pants to school. Well, we could wear them under our dresses, but we had to return our apparel to the girlish once inside the school doors. Presumably the no-pants rule existed to enforce ladylike demeanour, but miniskirts were all the rage in high school, and there was nothing less ladylike than less than a metre of cloth—unless it was the awfully named "hot pants." Perhaps it is obvious I attended Catholic schools (another factor in my life that flowed from my Cree grandmother, who was raised in a mission school). Forty years later, I still see girls in their private school uniforms hiking their little plaid skirts up to within an inch of their waists. My uniform-wearing days occurred in elementary school, and I could not have cared less what I had on at any time.

So what's the point, you ask? Well, clothes have a distinct effect on the female shape. Unless females walk around in muumuus (and even those are body type giveaways), whatever we put on screams something to the world. In my case, it was "flat ass." For many years, I could take off my hipster jeans without undoing them—I simply pulled them down my stick-straight body. No hips, no ass. I didn't sit down or even bend over at those parties my best friend dragged me to. First of all, I knew my jeans were likely to drift down and expose colossally unsexy cotton panties or sneakily slide off my non-existent hips and ass and puddle around my ankles. Second, I wasn't allowed to wear my glasses ("too dorky," according to best friend), so I tended to spend parties holding up a wall and my jeans until I could escape. I could easily flatten my entire body against a wall with no gaps. Not a one.

I remember girls in high school who lay on their beds, yanking on the zipper pull with pliers to get their jeans up. Why not just buy bigger jeans? I remember asking one friend, whose derision-laden response stifled that line of inquiry forever. I tried to resist most of the hormonally challenged antics of high school students with their dopey (yes, it's a pun) attempts at fun. Me—I'd always rather have been at home lying on my bed reading a book. High school parties tended to involve groups of teenagers inhaling bowls of chips while mumbling, "I can't feel anything. Are you off yet?" From my wall position, things looked quite dull and sounded even duller.

I still had little idea of the sexual attractions of the ass—other people's, that is. After all, *ass* leads to asinine, and *butt* was the butt of a joke. Shit came out of people's butts, and what was sexy about that? I had a thriving babysitting business when I was a girl, and, having changed countless diapers, I can say with complete certainty that dirty butts are not fun. When people cooed over the cuteness of little kids removing their clothes and running around butt-naked, I thought the adults were deranged—what could possibly be the attraction of an ass? Why were adults charmed by a photo of a naked baby on its stomach, butt in the air? (Well, not mine—it blended in with the rest of my baby blubber.) What's really depressing is the thought that someday someone may have to change my diapers. Again. One of my friends whose mother died from old age and Alzheimer's still has a Depends in the glove compartment of his car. Butts are messy—at all ages and sizes.

So I confess it was with shock that I realized asses were viewed with interest, and that they weren't necessarily supposed to be flat extensions of one's back progressing to one's legs, but rather were supposed to protrude in a perky, even saucy, manner. And they were to be shaken. In 1976, when I was an undergraduate, KC and the Sunshine Band released "(Shake, Shake, Shake) Shake Your Booty." I had to figure out what a booty was. I was under the impression booty was something pirates looked for. Imagine my surprise. And as a booty-less person, what could I do? Shake, shake, shake your boney butt—it just doesn't evoke the same nuance.

Also, shaking any body part calls attention to it, and as a teenager, I could annoy my mother by flipping my long hair around. Looking back, I realize that seeking attention for one's body was the first step to complete perdition, otherwise known as pregnancy. So in a convoluted way, having no booty to shake was a bit of birth control. The message we got was that anything sexual was (1) a sin and (2) unforgiveable. Catholic girls (probably all girls, for all I knew) were being told to think of sex as evil until marriage, and to then somehow become dutiful, even willing, partners to their husband's desires. But university in Alberta in the 1970s was a relatively free place sexually, thanks to the pill. Free to guys, that is. Girls still seemed to pay—either through pregnancy (no method of birth control is 100 per cent effective) or through broken hearts. By the time I made it out of university, three degrees and many years later, the fashions for all genders had become so sexualized or just downright silly that having a flat ass was practically irrelevant.

Things got worse in the Ass World as time went on: adults and children adopted the same clothing. Boys began wearing their jeans with the crotches starting at their knees, exposing their boxers or briefs. I imagined them using some kind of antigravity voodoo to keep from losing their pants altogether. Obviously, butts were not an issue for them. Girls started wearing jeans so low that my hipsters from high school were positively chaste by comparison, and they started displaying their thong underwear (whoever invented thongs, or whale tails as they are termed here on the West Coast, should have some seriously bad karma to deal with) and several feet of midriff. As one of my male friends pointed out, isn't the definition of an adult someone who can get their top and their bottom to meet? As usual, the more skin females flaunted, the better. For whom? I ask. The butt became more and more revealed—in your face, even.

As I aged, I discovered that many celebrities were admired for their booty. Jennifer Lopez and Beyoncé, to cite just two. I just thought their derrières looked big. How unhip of me. So I watched Beyoncé's YouTube clip of "If I Were a Boy." Yeah, right. Not even remotely possible, and while the big, beautiful voice wails about how badly boys treat girls, the shots of breasts and butts (all female) really play up the fact that we've come a long way, baby. Not. For one thing, we're still referred to as "baby," and let no one forget that the slogan was created to sell cigarettes. Beyoncé's clip had more than sixty-eight million hits when I watched it the first time—I just checked, and it now has half a million more hits.

Ah, so "junk in the trunk" is a good thing. Sort of. The online Urban Dictionary is a revelation to someone like me, who still uses paper—*The Canadian Oxford Dictionary* for regular, day-to-day use and the magnificent *OED* (in the go-blind edition with magnifying glass) when I really want to do some serious investigating. The Urban Dictionary provides an education: I learn that *badonkadonk* is one of the many synonyms for junk in the trunk, and the entry comes complete with an image and the info that deep booty cleavage is important. That certainly explains the disappearance of the thong between the butt cheeks. I also learn that assessments are all relative. There's too much junk in the trunk; there's SUV in the pants; there's even a description of a contest in which guys pool money in a bar (where else) and the winner—the guy who beds the female with the largest butt—gets the dough. It's called "nail the whale." And a skinny flat ass is anathema to booty lovers. Bottom line here: women's asses in whatever configuration are up for ridicule.

A few days ago I read an article in the *Globe and Mail* about a twenty-year-old woman named Claudia from London who flew to the United States to have her buttocks enhanced. She took the trip with a friend, and they had their buttocks injected with silicone by two women pretending to be surgeons. Apparently this was the second time Claudia had had the procedure. It would be the last time she would have any procedure. It went terribly wrong, and she died as a result of her desperate need to "fix" her body to meet some precise ideal of female attractiveness. It is possible to have real doctors do buttocks implants or protein injections, but these are expensive. According to the American Society for Aesthetic Plastic Surgery, buttock augmentation costs upwards of forty-two hundred dollars—and that price includes only the operation, not the anesthesia, hospital stay, or any other cost. Claudia had tried to save money. Her deadly injections cost a mere two thousand dollars.

Such longing for a particular body shape is tragic. Claudia is not the only woman to die from some form of buttocks augmentation. One of the most famous cases is that of Solange Magnano, a thirty-eight-year-old former Miss Argentina, who died in 2009 from complications after buttocks surgery, a procedure that she thought would be safe and simple. Given the risks, wearing padded panties to enhance one's rear seems more sensible. On July 23, 2010, Kelly Ripa of *Live with Regis and Kelly* showed off her padded panties—called Booty Pop panties. Fortunately she just held up a pair. Viewers were spared live modelling.

The desire for a "bubble butt" may be genetically encoded—in many cultures, the more rounded the woman's shape, the more fecund she is believed to be—but the extremes to which some women go in their body-shaping efforts is demeaning for everyone involved. That's the human race. It was ever thus. I think of the Elizabethans' insane hip-widening contraptions that forced women to enter rooms sideways or the Victorians' passion for bustles. Brassieres lift and shape, minimize, or even become lethal, cone-shaped weapons. Women have dumped girdles and embraced Spanx. What's the difference? Women (and men for that matter) are constantly bombarded by images of the ideal body shape. And the target keeps shifting. Contrary to those who aspire to heroin chic, it is possible to be too thin. You can die. It is also possible to be too fat. Same reason. And while a certain amount of lip service is paid to the notion that beauty comes in different shapes, few people pay attention. When it comes to thin, models set the bar for women, and the bar is impossible. So supermodel Heidi Klum hit the runway six weeks after giving birth. Such a quick recovery can make other new mothers feel like a complete failure and lead them to surgery. It sends me to the bar in search of a glass of Sauvignon Blanc—or possibly a bottle. The extra calories do not migrate to my ass, where some might say I could use them, but to my gut, which has more presence and bounce than my ass. Perhaps it's the freedom of middle age (okay, I'd have to live to be over a hundred to call this middle age) or my lifelong aversion to operations, injections, or funny clothes, but I simply don't care about having a flat ass. It's part of me—just like my big feet, my astigmatic short-sighted brown eyes, or my freckles.

It turns out that *Embracing Your Big Fat Ass* is like any other self-help book. Some cute lines, some reasonable advice—the title says it all. From an informal survey among male and female friends, I'd have to say that many women are far more likely to worry about having a big ass than a flat one. My best guy friend remarked that every woman he has ever been involved with (and let's just say the number is in the double digits) has asked him a variation of "Does this outfit make my ass look big?" And—always!— the correct answer is "No." Women ask each other the same thing. For proof, just eavesdrop on conversations in change rooms.

So at one extreme, women are supposed to have a bodacious booty and boobs, and at the other extreme women are considered better the less there is of them. As with all the other body parts, the ass is never neutral.

I am not going to embrace my flat Cree ass. I'm just going to live with it as I always have. For me, that means leisure time spent mostly lying on the couch or on the bed reading a book. That probably explains why the back of my head is flat too.

bones,
blood,
heart,
back . . .

Cage of Bones

Brian Brett

I was the lord of the wind, catching air, catching altitude, a roller boy before they called us roller boys. It was a summer in the early 1960s, somewhere around there, and I was alone, as thirteen-year-olds often like to be, fighting wind and gravity, grinding my roller skates into the asphalt, whistling down hills, leaping over the few speed bumps of that era. I thought I was beautiful and golden when I was flying—not the screwed-up, gimped kid that walked on strange legs.

I had wheels and I leaped and I twisted until the day I came down suddenly in the driveway. The pain went up my leg like a sexual thrill, and a dull throb followed, the cramping of my ankle, the paralysis. I managed to wrench the roller-boot off, and then I watched an alien inhabit my flesh, growing it, moulding it in front of my eyes. The sharp-edged ankle became a lumpy tumour, a swelling where the foot joined the ankle. And the pain never left, nor did the tumour. I didn't tell my parents. I just limped past them, grumbling about how I sprained my ankle on their cheap driveway. I was a cheeky, defiant one from the day I saw the first lights in the delivery room. It took forty years and an X-ray before I allowed myself to admit I'd broken my first beautiful bone.

Bone is a remarkable instrument. We normally have two hundred and six bones in our adult bodies, perhaps a few extra—depending on breakage. Children have several dozen more bones because they fuse together as we age. Children's bones are very soft. You will notice this by the way children bounce, mostly. The ones that don't bounce cause the guilt that a few people carry for life—after their children bounced badly when they were dropped or were backed over in the driveway.

I saw a nine-year-old child struck by a car once—called by his father to join him, he turned and dashed across the road to his father's car. When the oncoming vehicle hit him, the thump was chilling, and he flew thirty feet through the air, bouncing his head and chest off the gravel. The look of horror on the father's face is an image that will stay with me until I die. The child was still for a paralyzing moment; then he lifted his head like a snake testing the air while coming out of a burrow. He leapt to his feet and ran screaming to his daddy, only a few scratches from the gravel on his face. That kid bounced well.

> The foot bone connected to the leg bone,
> The leg bone connected to the knee bone,
> The knee bone connected to the thigh bone,
> The thigh bone connected to the backbone,
> The backbone connected to the neck bone,
> The neck bone connected to the head bone,
> Oh, hear the word of the Lord!
>
> Dem bones, dem bones gonna walk aroun',
> Dem bones, dem bones gonna walk aroun',

These are the words of the old American traditional folk song "Dry Bones," created to explain the biblical prophecy of Ezekiel 37:1–14 while simultaneously (and somewhat incorrectly) teaching anatomy to children. It's one of many variations since the 1800s—later put to music by James Weldon Johnson. I heard it when I was very young, and it stuck with me.

When I was a teenager my bones started to sing strange songs to me. They hurt. I didn't know it then, but I was suffering from a curious and rare disease called Kallmann syndrome. This made my bones grow oddly and my hips splay, giving me a feminine waist atop a whole lot of leg—legs that went down miles to the earth, it seemed, for such a tiny man—and I had arms like an orangutan. I also didn't know that the pain was a condition called osteoporosis. All my joints were wearing down, my bones hollowing out, bird-like, even as I was growing. And that's why, unconsciously, when I discovered Hector de Saint-Denys Garneau and his "Bird Cage" poem, I immediately understood it.

> I am a bird cage
> A cage of bone
> With a bird
>
> The bird in my cage of bones
> Is death making his nest

I was building my nest in my bones, or maybe it actually was death in my bones, but I never had much sympathy for death, and so I rushed into my life, leaping from grey log to log on the beaches of the coast, crevasse-jumping in the high mountains. Leaping . . . leaping . . . over death, denying the pain.

> Dem bones, dem bones gonna walk aroun',
> Dem bones, dem bones gonna walk aroun',

Then I was out in a duck field, a generally depressed torch of a twenty-five-year-old man. I was riding what I called the suicide express in those years. They'd diagnosed my syndrome by then and shot me up full of testosterone and sent me out into the world. Dumb move, really. Especially since they didn't have much knowledge of the proper dosage. So I was crazy and on steroids, riding that suicide express, my train to oblivion, taking risks such as standing in the middle of roads and watching drivers slam on their brakes and come to screeching stops. Then I'd calmly walk away while they had nervous breakdowns. That sort of thing. Sneaking up behind bears and scaring them. It was fun making a bear shit itself and run for its life.

So I was suicidal, but strangely not when I shot myself. The degeneration of my bones was slowing down. I was sober and in the glory of life. I was a twenty-five-year-old steroid-inflated young man gone duck hunting with my dad. Only we'd decided I should give him my good single-shot for his ratty old pump shotgun without a safety. We set up what's called a "fly." Me standing in my blind at one end of the field with the pump. Father and my older brother at the other end of the field in their blind with the single-shot and a double-barrel. It should have worked.

Actually, we hardly needed the blinds. There were so many ducks flying around I started feeling dizzy. I had several dead birds stuck in the back of my mackinaw.

Then I caught a twig in the barrel. Instinctively, I pumped the gun out and flicked the twig. I didn't hear the bang, but I soon noticed my hand was all black and there was a finger missing, a birdy-bone sticking out.

A flickering part of a second either way and I could have either lost my hand or missed myself entirely. This pissed me off because I wasn't even thinking of suicide in that beautiful moment under the blue sky in the empty potato-and-corn field. I was especially annoyed once I realized that, even though I had pumped the gun out, a shell had remained in the chamber. As I pulled the gun back to knock the twig out, the trigger must have caught on the head of a duck hanging out of the big back pocket of the mackinaw.

I was shot by a dead duck.

And he blew that bone into the field so far I couldn't find it—some duck probably took the final revenge and ate it. I've seen photos of a mallard eating a frog, so it's possible.

I had to walk a half-mile across that exquisite field—part dead potato leaf, part yellow corn stubble, under that bluest of blue skies—holding my bloody finger above my head like a Renaissance saint pointing to heaven so the blood wouldn't squirt.

After they whacked me full of Demerol I was almost ready to party; the doctor trimmed the bone with giant nail clippers, rounding it off. It's weird to watch someone whittling your bone down.

My father was sick about the wound and the bad gun, and he soon destroyed it. Despite being hazy with painkiller and hurt, I had to stay up playing cards with my family that night, proving that the blown-away finger didn't matter much.

This lost little limb changed my world. I finally understood I couldn't run faster than a speeding bullet, like most twenty-five-year-old men think they can. And I had a ghost to carry with me the rest of my life. A ghost finger, gesturing invisibly at the good and evil craziness of the world.

> The head bone connected to the neck bone,
> The neck bone connected to the backbone,
> The backbone connected to the thigh bone,
> The thigh bone connected to the knee bone,
> The knee bone connected to the leg bone,
> The leg bone connected to the foot bone,
> Oh, hear the word of the Lord!
>
> Dem bones, dem bones gonna walk aroun',
> Dem bones, dem bones gonna walk aroun',

Bones are the magical architecture of our lives. They protect our brains and our hearts. And, if you think about it, they offer us a peculiarly complex form of locomotion. After all, we could be oozing and slithering instead of walking. And they act as a kind of echolocation—reverberating within our flesh, adding to our deciphering of the ambient sounds around us—so not only can we knock bones together to make music, but our bones allow us to position ourselves within a crowd. In water the skull and neck bones sing to the bones in the ear. Yes, we actually do "hear it" in our bones.

Structurally, bones consist of an exterior of overlapping cross-grained cells that could provide a model for plywood, with a hard, smooth surface. Inside, they resemble soft crystals—honeycombs of trabecular tissue, a kind of spongy connectivity that consists of red and yellow marrow.

Both within the bone, and even on the bone's surface, all kinds of miracles occur daily. Hard exercise builds up the calcium and strengthens weak bones. Alcohol sucks the calcium out of the bones and makes them brittle. It's been suggested, as well, that the dehydrating effects of alcohol and coffee reduce the liquid buffer between the bones within the joints—damaging them over years of use. Hormones strengthen bones. That's why women lose bone structure when they go through menopause, and why I did when I was fifteen and generated no hormones.

And when the body goes bad, it can turn our flesh into bones. Fibrodysplasia ossificans progressiva (FOP) is a rare and deadly condition whereby the connective tissue gradually turns to bone until it encases the body. The most famous sufferer of this disease, Harry Eastlack, could move only his lips by the time he died shortly before his fortieth birthday.

Good bones don't just protect our brains and hearts, they also have magical abilities to filter our blood, create new blood, and remove heavy metals and toxins from the blood and store them. They adjust our pH, store heavy metals, assist our kidneys, and regulate our lymphatic system, blood sugar levels, and fat metabolism. They store calcium and phosphorus on their outer surfaces. Even more miraculously, they produce "multipotent" stem cells, essential to the body rebuilding itself, which is why they are used in bone marrow transplants.

Dem bones, dem bones gonna walk aroun',
Dem bones, dem bones gonna walk aroun',

Bones have many more uses. Animal bone marrow is delicious and healthy when cooked and has a terrific "mouth feel"—the reason why lamb or beef shanks are so tasty. There's a famous ballad, "The Old Woman from Wexford," about spousal murder that begins with a dangerous dish of egg and marrow bones.

Burnt bone, or bone ash, is used in the creation of the semi-luminous bone china now ubiquitous in our culture, though it was invented only a little more than two hundred years ago as a pseudo-form of Chinese porcelain. When I made pottery, I often used bone ash in glazes. There's a wonderful Chinese folk story about a potter, famous for his blue glazes, who was wood-firing his long dragon kiln, which had several joined chambers climbing up the hill above his studio. Suddenly a typhoon struck, but the determined potter, fearing that shutting down the firing would ruin the pots, kept stoking the kiln. During the chaos of the storm, a panicked pig rushed into a firing hole on the other side of the hill, and the apprentices didn't dare tell their master what had happened during their watch. Upon opening the kiln after it cooled, he discovered that most of the pots in one chamber were broken, though a few had survived, and these were a wonderful scarlet colour. The copper, calcium-infused glaze was no longer blue. Word of these miraculous ceramics soon reached the emperor who, when he saw them, immediately called for the potter. He purchased the pots and requested a dinner set with the same glaze. A request from the emperor was also a command.

The unfortunate potter went home and tried everything he knew, yet he could not duplicate the glaze. Several large firings proved negative. The emperor grew impatient and gave him an ultimatum. On the final day, the potter was still firing his climbing kiln, but he knew he wasn't going to be able to repeat the special colour. In despair, he threw himself into the giant stokehole at the base of the kiln. Many days later, when his mourning family and apprentices began to unload the kiln, they discovered that the pots in the chambers were the most exquisite red. The old master had thus accidentally fulfilled his mandate. By hurling a less burnable object into the stokehole, much smoke was created, which choked the atmosphere, turning it from oxidation to reduction, creating a complex chemical reaction with this sudden introduction of more copper, calcium, and bone ash released from the body of the potter, converting the copper in the glazes from blue to red, and thus creating the legendary oxblood glaze as it's known today.

Bone ash can also be converted into what's known as super-phosphate, which is especially valuable for fertilizer. Bones are surprisingly fertile. Bone meal can be a source of one of the holy trinity of chemical fertilizers first discovered more than a hundred years ago. Nitrogen. Phosphorus. Potassium. These three soon became the heart of the green revolution that swept the planet from the 1960s onwards, a revolution whose toxic aftermath we are now bathing in.

Bones were also used as a food supplement for livestock. This was the agri-business cycle that led to bovine spongiform encephalopathy (BSE), caused by feeding nutrient-rich bone, meat, and blood meal to herbivores. This "mad cow disease" also affects people, causing variant Creutzfeldt-Jakob disease, which destroys the nerves in the brain until the grey tissue begins to resemble a sponge. It's been speculated that the disease first moved into cattle that were fed rendered sheep infected with scrapie, a similar brain disease in sheep. It became evident in cattle once the new regime of the factory farms was promoted by so many governments in the Western world. It's thought that it transfers to humans through the ingestion of infected nervous tissue in meat, the sawn bone, and nerve tissue fragments from the spines of infected cattle. Feeding ground-up bones to animals was initially successful economically, like the green revolution, and then it became a repulsive act. It's now banned, though some people are probably already incubating variant Creutzfeldt-Jakob without knowing it. Today's farmers keep a lookout for any symptoms of aberrant behaviour in livestock, so BSE incidents have once again become as rare as being hit by lightning.

Ezekiel cried, "Dem dry bones!"
Oh, hear the word of the Lord.

I had been killing pigs with a farmer down the road, Mike Byron. Afterwards we were going to swap some chickens. We were walking up his muddy, goose-shit-slick driveway. I love Mike's farm, but it can be a death trap. I'd already dislocated my collarbone and cracked several ribs in falls outside of his smokehouse—balancing on the bent-legged aluminum chair we had to stand on to string up our hams, sausages, and fish—and I finally started bringing my own ladder.

His driveway was a standard, slimy, rainy West Coast road. I didn't give it much thought until I started slipping and slammed into a rock. I turned to Mike and said, "Look at that" or some such thing. He was aghast. My foot was turned sideways.

"Don't worry," I said, "I've got hard bones," not realizing that too many years of mountains and scotch had whittled them down. "I must have sprained it." I grabbed the foot and twisted it back into line. Then I kept on walking. It hurt a little, but I have a high pain threshold.

I gathered up my chickens. Oh, I'm a determined man. Then I drove off in my clunky, three-geared van, every push on the clutch sending electricity to my brain. It was a rush, as they say. By the time I reached home the shock had worn off; I could barely crawl down the entrance deck into the house, crying for Sharon, my wife: "I need help!" It's not something I say often, but I needed it then.

We got me shaved and cleaned up, exchanging all the pig's-blood-stained clothing for clean threads before she hauled me to the hospital. The doctor took one look at my X-ray and announced I'd set my broken leg perfectly; I wouldn't need any pins because it was now locked in by the swelling. He just threw a cast on and said, "Don't do that again! You were lucky." I could have set the bone wrong and that would have meant surgery. Then I was given what was becoming the traditional strong whack of Demerol, and I remember blissfully fading away, my blood full of sugary delight, temporarily wondering if I should break my bones more often, though I wouldn't recommend it.

The next time I didn't receive any Demerol. It was the even nastier, hateful morphine that made me feel dull and disguised the wracking pain of my stomach, which was mostly caused by the anti-inflammatories eating out my stomach wall, so that it felt exceptionally awful when I finally stopped needing the morphine. I'd worn the joints of both knees down so badly the doctors decided to replace one. This, more or less, consists of cutting your leg open, stapling all the muscles and whatever to some kind of board (or let me say, this is the image I created in my foggy, anesthetic-clogged brain), and then sawing off the knobs of your bones, gluing titanium joints to the ends, maybe adding a bolt or two, before putting everything back in place.

I woke up screaming in pain. In this age of cutbacks it took two hours for a nurse to arrive. She informed me I was consuming plenty of morphine from the push-the-button dispenser. I informed her even more professionally that in my tortured childhood I'd experienced more than enough drugs to know when I was receiving any painkillers. This didn't impress her. So I groaned the song of the bone-cutting knife and the stapler and the scalpels for almost a day until they grew fed up with my stupid, weakling complaints and decided to replenish my morphine supply. When they opened the case, all the unused morphine from the broken dispenser poured onto the floor. And they didn't have the grace to apologize.

Even though that was a bad patch, I've learned to live with pain, and think of her as a permanent companion, beautiful in her terrifying way, like an octopus in the blood, the dying nerves going numb or injecting sharp shots of agony.

One doctor wants to cut off my foot and praises the prostheses. Another wants to fuse the foot bones and throw in a few pins. He tells me that, if he cuts me up and rebuilds me, after one bedridden year, I will be able to walk half a mile without pain. Well, I can walk a lot farther than that with pain right now.

Thus I walk lovingly with these bones, knowing their history, knowing their mythology. Walking on my crumbling feet, the growing numbness and pain feels like walking across electrified needles. And my remaining knee feels like it's laced with broken teeth—which makes me recall Jason's bony enemies risen from the dragon's teeth that Cadmus had sown years earlier. Or Ezekiel's prophecy of the valley of dry bones. Or the skulls of a few long-dead animals that I keep as talismans beside my desk, along with a human skull carved out of wood that helps me remember Hamlet and the skull of his childhood jester: "Alas, poor Yorick! I knew him . . ." Perhaps my fascination with bones explains why I'm so fond of the sculptures of Henry Moore. He often used bones and stones as models for his monumental bronzes. Yet, mostly I keep returning to the prophecy of Ezekiel.

> The hand of the Lord was upon me, and . . . set me down in the midst of the valley which was full of bones, and caused me to pass by them round about: and, behold, there were very many in the open valley; and, lo, they were very dry.

And sometimes my thoughts go back further, and I remember Stanley Kubrick's film ape converting a bone into a weapon in *2001: A Space Odyssey*. Our fascination with bones has continued until today. The bones of the world stacked in ossuaries. The catacombs in Paris. The bone chapel at Our Lady of the Conception of the Capuchins in Rome. The skulls of Aboriginal peoples retained for display in museums. The skeletons of Halloween. The endless candy skulls of the Day of the Dead. John Donne's "A bracelet of bright hair about the bone." The terror-inducing skull-and-crossbones flag of pirates. And bone armies. Why do bone armies fascinate us?

I know of two major online computer games that include bone

armies. In the *Armies of Gielinor*, an Army of Bones is a major Achievement. Each player begins with twenty-five skeletons. If you turn your Mana up, you can have the skeletons come to your aid two or three at a time. You can also win other Achievements, such as Run Dwarves, Escape! I'm not making this up. The more complex game, *Dark Age of Camelot*, involves a series of Bone Army spells and sorcery rules so arcane that even long-time gamers appear to have trouble figuring them out.

It's likely that both games were inspired by the work of the brilliant stop-action animator Ray Harryhausen, who first embedded bone soldiers in our minds when Sinbad defeats a bone enemy animated by the evil sorcerer in *The 7th Voyage of Sinbad*, a battle so admired in the fantasy and animation world that Harryhausen upped the ante by having Jason and two soldier-companions sword fighting with eight skeletons in his masterpiece *Jason and the Argonauts*. Though according to the Greek myth the skeletons were defeated merely by rolling a precious stone between them, which set them fighting among themselves.

> Prophesy upon these bones, and say unto them, O ye dry bones . . . I will cause breath to enter into you, and ye shall live: and I will lay sinews upon you, and will bring up flesh upon you, and cover you with skin, and put breath in you, and ye shall live . . . there was a noise, and behold a shaking, and the bones came together, bone to his bone.
>
> . . . Come from the four winds, O breath, . . . and the breath came into them, and they lived, and stood up upon their feet, . . . an exceeding great army.

The bone armies of nightmares and movies. The bone armies of gamers—they are always threatening us. The "Dry Bones" song quoted earlier is an amusing nursery song that, interestingly, forgets that Ezekiel's army dashes out the brains of the children of its enemy.

In the bone caves of Battambang, in Cambodia, an old, shaven-headed woman ties a red cotton thread around my wrist and blesses me after I put money in her donation box, one of dozens littering the site where the Khmer Rouge took their victims, shot them in the back of the head, and pushed them through the sinkhole to the caves below. Some victims didn't die for days, groaning in the pile of rotten bodies and bones. Now the skulls are stacked in a little altar that a monk will gracefully open for you. Another donation box is placed obviously nearby. In the brief period of Khmer Rouge ascendancy in the 1970s, uncounted innocents died here. Then the Vietnamese Army arrived and set up howitzers on nearby Crocodile Mountain, and the two armies exchanged nightly rounds just to make sure the other side knew they were still there, until the night the Khmer Rouge slipped into the darkness.

The caves were soon colonized by a group of Buddhists, who decided to venerate the victims rather than burn their remains according to custom. Every year, as more bones rise to the surface, they are collected and separated into their appropriate pile, according to their estimated age and sex. Did I mention there were donation boxes, many donation boxes? They are used to build more temples funded by tourists who need to be reminded what tragedy is.

Choeung Ek, one of the infamous Killing Fields, saw the most executions during the Khmer Rouge terror. It is now a memorial a few kilometres outside the capital city of Cambodia, Phnom Penh. There is a tower of skulls several storeys high, also separated according to age and sex. Not far away is the killing tree, where the executioners picked up children by the legs, swung them around, and dashed their heads against the tree trunk, which now has a large burl, nurtured by the tree's wounds and the blood and bones and brains of children.

A few yards away on a dusty trail is another killing site. Every year the monsoons come and go, the rain and the erosion revealing a new layer of bones. We are told they are solemnly collected and stored. Staring at the bones erupting from the bare soil of the killing site made me think of Jason's dragon teeth.

This entire monument to the dead has now been leased to JC Royal, a Japanese corporation that apparently specializes in entertainment attractions. A trip to the Killing Fields helps us recognize why our species is now capable of eventually turning the entire world into killing fields.

Back in a Phnom Penh suburb, a school that was converted into the main detention camp for prisoners has also been preserved. We learn that they used to play loud music to muffle the screams. The torture tools are nakedly displayed, along with photos of the victims. Room after room of them. The skulls of many of the victims, all inside a glass case, are obviously dusted regularly. Some are varnished. The bullet holes in the skulls are so tiny. They look about the size of a .22 shell. When the management of the camp had to perform mass killings, which was almost every night, they would truck the victims away in the dark to the killing site at Choeung Ek. Sometimes there were several trucks.

It's endlessly fascinating how we absorb our grim histories, even pay to view the bones left behind. Despite the horror of the Killing Fields, many people, like and unlike me, line up to buy tickets.

After an hour wandering in Choeung Ek and finally ending up back at the dragon's teeth, it suddenly occurred to me that this soil would be extremely fertile. I was flooded with the strange thought that in some other time long ahead, maybe some young farmer will discover a field unnaturally rich with minerals and the cycle will begin again.

Dem bones, dem bones gonna walk aroun',

Despite our erratic and dangerous history as a species—our bone-breaking ways—I still love us as a wonder of creation . . . and my own dangerous bones. They are beautiful despite my mistreatment.

I have broken them and torn their cartilages and tendons so badly that one thigh filled with black blood for a year. And now, though they are killing me with pain, I still sing through them. Sometimes I think I can hear them singing back at me, after all these years. Sing, my bones!

I also talk to my bones when we go walking, and they talk back, crackling their sad notes of age and disease and pain when once they sang about the run and the leap across those near-bottomless crevasses overlooking the Mamquam glacier in the Coast Range, the glory of the cold wind in my hair as my bones braced me when I landed after every leap. Alive! Alive!

We understood each other, my bones and I—during those days—and still do. We're going to keep going to the end of the road, and even then, we will merely transmigrate together. We will be fertile again. We will be cremated. We will become ashes. Oxblood on the ceiling of the crematorium. Red hearted and alive. And dust to be scattered in the ocean of life.

Blood Typing

Susan Olding

It made sardonic sense that my father—a pathologist—would develop a rare blood disorder. Waldenström's macroglobulinemia is a slow-growing non-Hodgkin lymphoma that begins in white blood cells called B-lymphocytes. B cells, which form in the lymph nodes, spleen, and bone marrow, are an important part of our immune systems; some B cells mature into plasma, which contains the antibodies that protect us from viruses and bacteria. In Waldenström's, abnormal lymphoplasmacytic cells multiply out of control, producing large amounts of a protein called monoclonal immunoglobulin M antibody, or IgM. High levels of IgM in the blood cause hyperviscosity—sludgy blood. The very mechanism that is supposed to protect the body turns against it.

"There's no cure," Dad told me. "But they can treat it for a while." He was stoic and matter of fact, and this was characteristic of him (although after he died, my mother told me that on the day he heard the diagnosis, he wept like a child).

Then he consulted his texts. As a man, he may have trembled at the prospect of mortality, but as a born researcher, he loved more than anything to learn. The likelihood of being struck with this disease is six in a million. What better excuse to hit the books? He knew his prognosis and had figured out the treatment protocol before he even met his hematologist. It was almost like coming out of retirement.

As his blood thickened, Dad suffered from weakness, fatigue, bruising, bleeding from the gums, loss of appetite, and loss of weight. His vision sometimes blurred, he got headaches, he felt dizzy, and his legs became so heavy he could barely lift them. He didn't speak about any of this. Yet his legs especially bothered him. His circulation had never been good; for as long as I could remember he'd worn heavy elastic socks for his varicose veins.

Treatment included chemotherapy, with rituximab and cyclophosphamide, combined with corticosteroid drugs such as prednisone. The side effects of these drugs are less obvious than for some other forms of chemotherapy, but long-term use of steroid drugs can lead to osteoporosis.

My parents lived in a suburban split-level house with many stairs. Dad refused the indignity of a cane. And every evening, for decades, he drank to the point of intoxication. He often stumbled.

For a long time, with my mother's help, or my brother's, or, once, a paramedic's, Dad managed to get back on his feet after his falls. His hockey-playing youth may have lent him some protection against early bone loss; on the other hand, his diet had never been good, and now that he wasn't hungry, it was even worse. Add the risks of prednisone, and it's a miracle he didn't break a bone much earlier.

When he finally did, it was his hip. He would have to undergo surgery for a replacement. There wasn't much I could do to help, but I wanted to be with my family, so I made the four-hour trip from Kingston to west of Toronto to sit with my mother and brother in the tiny room where, two years earlier, my brother and father and I had sat out my mother's mastectomy.

We waited. And waited. An orderly had promised that someone would come to tell us when the surgery was over. We stared at the cool blue walls and leafed through magazines that had not changed since our last visit. Outside, the sun shifted position in the sky; inside, other families came and went. My brother and I paced, stopping at the pamphlet rack. "One in four elderly patients die within a year of their first fall," we read—wordlessly agreeing to keep that grim statistic from our mother.

Visiting hours ended and the lights in the hallway dimmed and still we sat there. Finally my brother went to investigate. Dad was resting in his own room. He had come through the operation without difficulty, but no one had remembered to fetch us. Another man might have spoken up and asked where we were. But not Dad.

Blood can be classified in a number of ways, but the most common is the ABO system, discovered in 1901 by Austrian-born pathologist Karl Landsteiner. Landsteiner began with a simple question: why did blood transfusions sometimes save patients and sometimes kill them? Using samples from his colleagues, he separated their cells from their serum and suspended the red blood cells in a saline solution. Then he mixed each individual's serum with a sample from every cell suspension. Some mixtures clotted, while others did not.

Landsteiner's experiment persuaded him that red blood cells could be grouped according to their tendency to clump in the presence of specific serums, and he called these groups A, B, and O. (His co-workers later identified a fourth group, AB.) The names A, B, AB, and O refer to the different kinds of antigens on the surface of the red blood cells. An antigen is a substance that triggers the production of an antibody by the immune system. People with A type blood have A antigens on their red blood cells. Those with B type blood have B antigens. People with AB type blood have both A and B antigens, and people with O type blood have neither A nor B antigens.

Normally, our bodies do not make antibodies against molecules they recognize. So people with type A blood do not make antibodies against the A antigen, which is already present in their blood. But they do make antibodies against the B antigen. If someone with type A blood receives type B blood during a transfusion, his or her antibodies will attack the B antigen on the donated red blood cells. This is what causes the blood to clump, or agglutinate, and agglutination may prove fatal.

In the year before my father broke his hip, I had not seen him.

I had written an essay that spoke about his drinking, and I had published the essay in a book. He was angry—as angry as he'd ever been—and he forbade me to enter my parents' house. My husband and daughter and I were no longer welcome there. He would not speak to me, he would not speak about me, and he did not want to hear my name.

My mother told me all this over the phone. She waited until he had gone out because she didn't want him to know she'd made the call. I sat down—I had been standing—and stared out our back window at a leaden February sky. "I'm sorry," she said. Her voice shook with the effort to get it out. "I know what you meant—but he doesn't." She understood that I had written out of love, not anger, and that I hadn't intended to hurt my father; after all, I had dedicated the book to the two of them. But even though she believed he was wrong, she would not question his decision. If he wanted to shut me out of his life, she knew him too well to argue.

In the first weeks after her call, I felt guilty and ashamed. Who did I think I was, writing about a part of my dad's life that he had never acknowledged? Couldn't I have kept it to myself? These things are *private*, I could hear my mother saying, just as she had said when I was a teen. And he is old, and sick, and frail. Why add to his stress in this way? After all, if I hadn't *intended* to hurt him, I'd recognized that by publishing, I *might* hurt him. Surely I had blood on my hands.

But as the months dragged on, I would think about my nine-year-old daughter, robbed of any relationship with her grandparents. I would think of my brother, caught uncomfortably between my father and me. I'd think of my mother, virtually housebound for decades because of an eye disorder, and now even more isolated, left without the comfort of my calls and visits. And I would think about what I had written—not an exposé, but an exploration of all I owed to my father; not a damning indictment, but a clear-eyed tribute. Then my blood would boil.

For as long as I'd known him, my father had used silence as weapon and shield. So I shouldn't have been surprised by his decision to shut me out. Yet I *was* surprised, and also bewildered, because to me, this wordless cut-off seemed a dozen times more shameful than anything I had written about him. Could he not see how he was hurting the rest of us? Could he not feel that he was hurting himself? Why, after wilfully ignoring my writing for years, had he chosen to pick up the book? Had he even read the whole thing, or did he stop at the parts that bothered him? And if he was angry with me, why couldn't he discuss it, like an adult? But that was an idle wish. Expecting my father to talk about his feelings was like trying to wring blood from a stone.

Because my dad would have nothing to do with me, I couldn't call him or send him a letter. And anyway, what would I say? I couldn't apologize for writing what I'd written, because I wasn't sorry for that. I *was* sorry to have hurt him, but he would never have believed it. *Bloody-minded*, my mother would have said of both of us.

Righteous anger, profound loss, useless regret, stubborn conviction—I could isolate each of these feelings if I tried. But mostly they roiled around together and the whole thing felt like a bloody mess.

The recognition of ABO blood types revolutionized medical care. For the first time in history, transfusions became safe and reliable. So when Karl Landsteiner received the Nobel Prize in Physiology or Medicine, no one felt inclined to quarrel with the judges' decision.

Yet for all the importance of the ABO system, here in North America most of us rarely give our blood type a thought. It's a notation on the medical chart—nothing more. In Japan, things are different. There, many people believe that ABO blood type predicts personality, compatibility, suitability for various professions, and more. This belief can be traced to one Takeji Furukawa, a professor at the Tokyo Women's Teacher's School, who in 1927 published a paper called "The Study of Temperament Through Blood Type" in the scholarly journal *Psychological Research*. Despite Furukawa's lack of scientific credentials, the idea gained popularity, especially with racists, and the militarist government of the time commissioned a study in an attempt to breed the ideal soldier.

The theory that blood type determined temperament lost official favour in Japan during the 1930s as its lack of scientific grounding became apparent. But in the 1970s, a new wave of interest began. And as recently as 2008, a series of books describing personality by blood type crowded the Japanese bestseller lists in the third, fourth, fifth, and ninth positions.

The Japanese fascination with blood types is similar to the North American penchant for horoscopes—except that the Japanese take blood typing much more seriously. Stars typically mention their blood type for the benefit of their fans, and manga characters are given blood types by their creators. But more significantly, matchmakers use blood type to determine compatibility, and employers ask for blood type on job applications. There is even a form of blood type harassment, called *bura-hara*, which has been blamed for the bullying of children in playgrounds, the loss of professional opportunities, and the breakup of happy relationships.

Dad's fall broke the impasse between us. I arrived a day before his hip replacement. I had written him a note expressing my love and concern. My mother and brother gave him the card while I waited in the hospital corridor. I didn't want to force myself on him. I didn't want to upset him. We weren't even sure if he'd take the card, and if he refused it, I planned to go away. But he accepted it, and then he agreed to see me.

He lay propped up in the hospital bed. He wore a royal blue corduroy shirt that I had given him one Christmas. I took his hand. There was no anger in his face or in his manner. He was the same as always. Quiet and watchful. Perhaps a bit wary—but then, he'd always been wary with me. Maybe with everyone.

"What time's the operation?" I asked.

He brightened. Where many people might dread the prospect of surgery and dislike talking about it, Dad was in his element. "They have to replace it," he said. "I'll be down there for a while." He gestured to the bed. "Don't let anybody take my luxury spot here while I'm gone."

We laughed. He ate one of the Mars bars—favourites of his—which we had brought him, and we worked on the crossword puzzle together. It was as if the events of the past year had never happened.

Thank god, I thought. "Thank god," said my mother and my brother on our drive home, after we left him for the evening. The long stalemate was over. I was officially returned to the fold.

But if I mostly felt relief, I was also conscious of some residual irritation. All that worry, all that guilt, all that anger—for what? Because once again, we were playing by *his* rules. *Don't mention it*, he'd often say, brushing away thanks for some characteristically generous gesture. The phrase might have served as his motto. But now, in this context, his intractable silence felt to me like distance, avoidance, denial.

As a family, we showed the typical North American attitude to blood types. Even my father, with his professional interest in the subject, could not recall his own type when put to the test. One of the treatments for Waldenström's is a specialized type of transfusion, and while in hospital he received a few of these. "As long as your doctor knows what type you are," we joked.

My mother was the exception. "I may not know *his* type," she said, jerking her head in my dad's direction. "Or yours, or your brother's. But I do know mine." She is O negative—the so-called universal donor. In Japan, O is considered the best type of blood. Os are called "warriors." They are flexible, and sociable, loyal, ambitious, independent, and they always speak their minds. They value others' opinions, like to be the centre of attention, and are extremely self-confident.

Does this description fit my mother? It's hard to say. I never knew her before her marriage. And in marriage, as Donne reminds us in his poem "The Flea," "two bloods mingled be."

The hospital where my dad was a patient was the same hospital where, for more than twenty years, he had served as chief pathologist. In the weeks following his hip surgery, my brother and I sometimes wondered if the staff had entered into a conspiracy with him. It was impossible to get information from them. How long might he be kept there? What was his prognosis? Would he be expected to return home after his stay? Did they know about his drinking problem? Did they know that to send him home might be to return him to the bottle? He would need help bathing and dressing and using the bathroom. He would need help on the stairs. How could my blind and arthritic mother manage him?

It seemed there was no one who would answer these questions for us. It often seemed as if there was no one available to *ask*. His family doctor and the social worker did not return our calls. The nurses changed with baffling frequency. And we couldn't ask my dad. Or rather, we *could*, but he would only shrug and show us the back of his hand.

As my brother and I spiralled into worry, Dad got better. On morphine, he was more cheerful than he'd ever been on rum. He ate more than he had eaten in years. Warm colour flooded his cheeks. He quizzed us on a dozen different subjects, besting our knowledge every time. He even struck up a sort of friendship with the man in the bed next to his.

First he stood. Then he walked. Then he went home.

Dad managed at home for about two months before he fell again. In hospital, they X-rayed him and told him he was fine. But he knew he was not fine, and when the pain became too sharp for even him to bear in silence, my brother took him back. It turned out that he had broken his pelvis. They had examined only his hip. "Most common mistake in the ER," a physician friend later told me. "They do it all the time."

He was understandably angry, but he did not complain. He hated to admit to any failings in the medical system; in fact, he identified so strongly with his role as doctor that to him, a failure in the system implied a failure of the self. So perhaps predictably, in the days that followed, his anger turned inward. This time, he did not eat the hospital food and he did not eat the treats we brought him. He said it hurt him too much to try to get up; he was polite, but he would not do what the physical and occupational therapists asked of him. He looked ashen, irritated, and exhausted. When I called him on his eighty-fifth birthday, he wouldn't—or couldn't—muster the energy to say a simple hello to his granddaughter. And when we visited, he barked at us unexpectedly, or shook his head and waved us away. "Thanks for coming," he'd say. *Now get lost*, he didn't have to add.

We watched with concern as he grew weaker. His doctors shared our worry. "I'll give him another dose of the steroids," said his hematologist. The steroids tended to boost his appetite and energy. "I'll increase the antidepressant," his family doctor said. But nothing seemed to make a difference.

Of course he didn't talk about it. And to me, it seemed that he was abdicating. Letting his life slip away—without consciousness, without purpose, without a word.

According to the Japanese, people with type A blood are earnest, sensible, and responsible. Calm in crisis, they nevertheless tend to avoid confrontation, and they can be shy, withdrawn, and uncomfortable around others. They are also very artistic—the most creative of all the blood types. Stubborn perfectionists, type As often suffer from stress and they can be nasty drunks.

Type Bs are strong and passionate. When they initiate a project they give it their full attention; they tend to stick to their goals and follow them to the end, even if the result looks impossible. They like to follow their own rules and ideas, so they can be less than co-operative. Also, they live more in their heads than in their hearts, so they can sometimes appear cold, selfish, or unforgiving to others.

AB is considered the worst blood type, because it mixes qualities from both ends of the spectrum. Type ABs are the humanists. They feel deeply but are ruled by the head and not the heart, and therefore appear cool, controlled, and rational. They can also be forgetful, indecisive, and critical. At the same time, more than other types, they are capable of holding grudges.

Which type was my father? The shy, withdrawn, and stubborn A? After all, he *was*, at times, a nasty drunk. Or was he a B—goal-directed, fixated on his own aims, uncooperative and selfish? Then again, he could as easily have been an AB, with his appearance of calm control, his deep humanism, and his capacity to nurse a grudge.

And which type, I wondered, was I?

The history of Dad's second fall came to me in fragments. Against his therapist's orders, and without my mother's knowledge, he had gone out to the garage. When he fell, landing on his back, he hit the horn of his car with his cane to get her attention, but she didn't hear it. So he lay there, possibly for hours, before a neighbour finally discovered him.

I should have known what he was after: rum. My brother had refused to buy it for him, my aunt had refused to buy it for him, and my mother couldn't drive. So he went for it himself. And got it. It was on his way back that he lost his balance. That explained how he had managed to strike the horn while flat on his back; the car door was open. Bottles, car door, cane—together they were too much for him to manage. So the bottles crashed down with him. Luckily—or perhaps unluckily—they were plastic and didn't break.

At first, I was furious. We'd convinced ourselves, or hoped, that his first hospital stay would have weaned him from his addiction. We'd believed he would see that he was better off without it. But the moment his energy returned, the moment he had a chance, he was off like a naughty boy behind my mother's back. *He cares more for alcohol than he cares for any of us*, I thought. *He cares more for alcohol than he cares for his own health, for his own life! Yet he cannot and will not face the fact, and blames me for bringing it to his attention.* And my anger burned.

Yet whenever I envisioned him on that concrete floor, my heart collapsed. I could not imagine a better hell for him—to be helpless on his own ground, helpless because of a choice that he had made. And now I wondered, was he depressed because he knew that he could not go back to his old life, was he depressed because he felt ashamed of himself, or was he depressed because he wanted one last drink?

Although North Americans in general do not subscribe to the blood type theory of personality, a recent diet book, *Eat Right for Your Type*, suggests that people belonging to different blood groups may be better or worse adapted to specific foods, and that eating a diet suited to one's blood group may result in less illness, discomfort, and obesity. Naturopathic doctor Peter D'Adamo, originator of the diet, argues that type Os, the "warriors," are the oldest group, in an evolutionary sense; they are the consummate meat eaters. Type As, the "farmers," can do well on vegetarian fare. Type Bs, he claims, are descended from Mongolian hunters and do best without the farmer's staples of wheat, buckwheat, and oats. And type ABs, combining features of both A and B types, should focus on seafood, tofu, and green vegetables.

There's no scientific evidence in support of the blood type diet, but the various blood types *have* been associated with different diseases. When it comes to infectious diseases, type As seem more likely to contract smallpox, type Bs are more vulnerable to infantile diarrhea, and type Os are more susceptible to bubonic plague. They may also be tastier to mosquitoes, which could in turn make them targets for malaria.

The ABO phenotype has also been associated with certain non-infectious diseases. Gastric cancer is more common among type As, while ulcers are more frequent in type Os, and diabetes occurs more often among types O and A. But as far as I know, no one has tried to link blood group with the non-Hodgkin lymphomas such as Waldenström's macroglobulinemia.

One night I dreamed that I spoke to my father. "You have a choice," I told him. "You can enjoy what is left to you or you can fade away. What part of yourself are you going to honour in this hour? What part of yourself are you going to leave in the memories of the people you have loved?"

He was angry with me, of course. He fumed and he sputtered. He turned his face away and set his lips in a line. But then he got up. He paced the hospital hallway in his flimsy gown. The gown fell open at the back, but still he walked, his true dignity intact, even with his sorry old ass hanging out, all wrinkled and bony. He walked outside to the garden where the smokers sat, pushing the walker slowly but with pride. Then he sat and soaked the sunlight in—letting himself feel what he was losing, knowing he had the strength to bear it.

After months of stasis, the hospital team called a "family meeting." I couldn't be there because of the distance, but my mother and my brother went. The meeting opened with a question—the question we'd all been longing to ask. What did my father want?

"I want to go home," he said.

One by one the social worker, the doctors, the physiotherapist, the occupational therapist, my mother, and my brother all told my father why that couldn't happen. He couldn't stand, he couldn't use the bathroom, he wasn't eating, he wasn't strong enough.

But still, "I want to go home."

"All right, then," his family doctor, Dr. B., said. "But you'll have to co-operate. You'll have to work for it. Can you commit to that? To trying to get up? If you can, we'll discuss it again in two weeks."

My father agreed. And then Dr. B. threw a curve ball. "You told me," he said, "that the reason you're in here again is the rum. So what are you going to do about that?"

My mother and brother sat there, mouths agape. The doctor knew about my father's drinking; more than that, he knew the reason for my father's fall. That meant my father had spoken to the doctor and told him the story. "He's never spoken of it before," my mother told me later. "Never . . . admitted it like that." She paused. "I couldn't believe it."

Blood type is inherited. If you know the blood type of two parents, you can determine the possible blood types of their children, and if you know the blood type of one parent and one child, you can work backwards to establish the possible blood types of the other parent. For example, if one parent is type A and the other is type AB, their children will have blood types A, B, or AB. If one parent is type O and the child is type A, the other parent must have type A or type AB blood.

My father did make an effort for a day or two. He got dressed. He got up. But then he developed a fever and a cough. His doctors wanted to give him antibiotics, but he refused them. I think that's when I realized that I'd been wrong. He wasn't abdicating; he wasn't fading away. He had decided. Without control and independence, life was meaningless to him, so he was taking control of the only thing he could. They offered him food; he turned away from it. They asked him to get up, but he would not. He had never wanted to *talk* about his choices. He had only wanted to *make* them. Now he was making his final choice. His was death with dignity, after all.

Weekends, when I was a child, my dad would sometimes take me to the lab. He'd put on his white coat and stare at slides through a microscope. His expression sharpened and brightened when he was there; he looked alert and alive. Filled with purpose, I think now. Every slide was a fresh mystery. What would he find?

Often, he invited me to share in the discovery. He'd pull up another stool and show me how to adjust the lens. I stared through the eyepiece to another universe. "There," he pointed. "Those are the white cells. Those are the red. What do you notice about them? Compare them to this slide of normal blood."

How could he see meaning in these swirling purple blotches? How could he read them? And yet he could—he could.

I ordered the Eldon Blood Typing Kit from a company called WiseGeek. It came within a week, neatly packaged in a slim brown envelope. I put it to one side, telling myself that I would get to it in a day or two. Then I buried it among some other papers and forgot about it. Tried to forget about it.

What was I waiting for? Why was I resisting? After all, I knew that the lancet would only prick for a second. How badly could that hurt?

I saw my father for the last time a week before he died. I'd been visiting for a few days but needed to return for work and for my daughter; I'd be driving back home that afternoon.

When my mother and I arrived at the hospital, Dad's bed was curtained off. Beneath the curtain's hem we saw men's shoes and pant legs. "He's talking to the doctors," one of the nurses told us.

We made our way to the visitors' lounge, an unpleasant room bisected by a long table, with chairs lined up awkwardly around its perimeter and a blaring wide-screen TV. My mother sat down while I searched in vain for the remote. A few minutes passed and then my father's family doctor came in with a young resident. They shut the door behind them.

"Finally," said Dr. B. This was the first time I had seen him. He was tall and white-haired. He looked shrewd but not unkind.

"*Finally*, I've been able to get instructions from him." Spoken like a man who had long been frustrated in his aim.

We waited.

"He has agreed that from this point on, we are talking about palliative care."

We all looked at my mother, perhaps unconsciously expecting her to break down. Instead, she rose from her chair. "I knew that," she said. "No extraordinary measures." She smiled and stretched out her hand to Dr. B. as if to comfort him.

Dr. B. met my eye.

"That's consistent with what I know of my dad."

The doctor raised an eyebrow and shook his head. "*You* might have known it," he said. "But I didn't. He wouldn't talk to me, and I needed to have instructions."

My father would be transferred to the fourth floor, Dr. B. said, just as soon as the paperwork had been arranged.

"Does he know that?" my mother asked.

"Not yet. You can tell him, or I will."

"He'll know what that means," my mother mused. "He used to joke about it. Well, not joke, exactly . . . but you know: 'Nobody ever comes off the fourth floor alive.'"

She didn't want to be the one to break the news, so together the four of us trooped back to my father's room. Dad startled at our approach. He was so thin. His gums receded from his teeth and his skin stretched like oiled paper over a drum. "That isn't him," my mother would say later on. "It's not him anymore." We must have seemed enormous to him, and overwhelming—four sets of eyes, four looming faces, four big bodies crammed into such a tiny chamber. With its pale pink curtain and the green walls, it felt like the inside of a shell.

Dr. B. was brief. My father listened. "Fourth floor." He nodded and wiped a blue-veined hand across his brow. "No extraordinary measures." His voice sounded hoarse. Now he was silent not only from habit and from preference. It cost him tremendous effort to speak.

The doctors left then. Within minutes, a nurse bustled in with some papers that she wanted my mother to sign. I pulled up a chair. Looking into my father's eyes, I took his hand and squeezed. With whatever strength remained to him, he squeezed in return.

That was the closest we could come to an acknowledgment of love for each other. The closest we could come to goodbye.

Just then, my mother called me. The print on the forms the nurse was showing her was too small for her to decipher and she wanted help. I got up to go to her, but as I moved away, I could sense that my father was unhappy. From the corner of my eye I saw him shift in the bed and grimace.

I went back to him. "Can I do something, Dad?"

He jerked his chin in the direction of the curtain, still closed around the sides of his bed, blocking most of his view. "Open," he said. "I want it open."

How tempting to read this as a metaphor—to see it as a sign that he had finally found a way to loosen his tourniquet of shame.

The instructions looked forbidding. A page-long list of warnings. Ten separate steps, each with numerous sub-steps. But really, it was simple. Put a bit of water onto each of the test strips. Prick your finger with the lancet. Use a stick to get blood from your finger onto a test strip, and mix this around with water. Use a new stick to get blood for the next test strip, and so on until there is blood in each of the test strips. Wait for a few minutes, watch for agglutination, and read the results.

Blood itself—the sight of it—has never bothered me. As a kid, I could scrape a knee or slice my finger without a blink; a few years later, I slit open the frog in biology class without a second thought. One year, to pay my university tuition, I even took a job in a butcher's shop; I stood at a maple chopping block singing carols while disembowelling turkeys for the Christmas rush.

But I've never liked the thought of blood rivering through veins.

Even to write that makes me feel it—a crawling ache beneath the skin. Like being twisted inside out. Whenever I was forced to give a sample, I'd have to breathe deeply and close my eyes, just to keep the fear at bay.

Not anymore. A few weeks after my father died, I had to go for some tests. I chose an early morning hour. When I got there, the place was quiet and almost empty; they took me right away. I hung up my coat, pulled off my cardigan, and laid my arm on the melamine slab. This time I watched as the nurse plumped for a vein, watched as the needle sank in, kept watching as the ruby liquid filled the vials—one, two, three, four—all rubber-capped and ready for analysis.

That dream about my father, I see now, was really a message to myself. *Look at what you are losing. You have the strength to bear it.* He was a distant man, a prickly man, a complicated man, and our relationship was never easy. Yet I am so lucky in his legacy. Curiosity, determination, pleasure in discovery, a knack for finding patterns—they're in the blood.

Dad never asked me not to write about him again. He could never have spoken the words—and probably he knew that I could never have promised.

That's the type I am.

A Serious Arteriopath

Kate Pullinger

As I stood in my kitchen in my pyjamas, life swirled around me: my children, my husband, and our two houseguests were getting ready for school, getting ready for work, getting ready to leave. I was tired, not quite awake, and I had a headache; the new dean at the university where I worked part-time had decided to shut down the successful master's program I had spent the previous three years building and developing; my eleven-year-old son, a well-behaved and cautious boy, was in trouble at school for getting in a fistfight. My houseguests, one from Vancouver and the other from Toronto, were two of my oldest and closest friends, and they were both leaving that morning to go home to Canada.

My eight-year-old daughter was saying something to me. "Mummy?" She sounded annoyed. I turned to look at her; she was standing right beside me and I had not seen her. Puzzled, I looked away. Then I looked back. There was a gap in my peripheral vision—an entire region on my right side was missing. I turned my head to look at her straight on and she appeared; I looked to one side of where she was standing and she disappeared. I held up my right hand like a pupil in class and moved it up and down, forwards and back, but I could not see it.

When you fall in love, you feel it in your whole being, but it is your heart that swells, that beats too fast, that makes you feel light-headed and a little faint. I fell in love with my husband at the opera when he leaned close and touched my arm lightly. My heart thumped so loudly I could no longer hear the music.

OUTPATIENT DEPARTMENT—GERIATRIC SERVICES—March 7, 2001
REASON FOR REFERRAL:
Assessment of increasing functional incapacity due to multifactorial problems.

HISTORY OF PRESENT ILLNESS:
This fine gentleman was accompanied by his daughter, who says that he is at Saanich Peninsula Hospital for respite right now. His primary caregiver, i.e., his wife of fifty-two years, has gone on a vacation. She is feeling really over-burdened by his dependency, which is functional and psychological. This man has poor visuospatial capacity, resulting in numerous falls and increasing needs for personal care. This seems to have come on in a progressive way over the last ten years. The daughter is unable to identify any one particular time when he may have had stroke disease, though he is a serious arteriopath. She has wondered about a series of strokes because of his increasing word-finding difficulty, short memory loss, urinary dysfunction, and swallowing disorder. He has had previous urinary problems with bladder neck contracture in 1992, and he is now voiding up to twenty times at night and has been recently put on a trial of antibiotics for a recurrent UTI. There has been the provisional home support working overnighting every other night at the house, which is helping to some degree, but the burden is really growing and the question is whether there is any remediable dimension to unburden caregivers and make this fellow's quality of life a bit better.

I stood there moving my hand back and forth, in and out of the gap in my peripheral vision, with my daughter getting more and more annoyed with me as I continued to ignore her question. I turned my attention to breakfast and packed lunches for school and other such things, but I kept returning to this movement, moving my right hand up and down like a malfunctioning robot, until my husband asked me what I was doing. I kept my voice low so that the kids wouldn't hear. What could this gap in my peripheral vision mean?

Was I going blind?

The kids left for school, my husband left for work, and my two houseguests and I sat down around the kitchen table for our final conversation before they left for Heathrow. I mentioned the gap. They looked at me, horrified. I explained that it was not a black hole but rather an empty space—my brain was doing its duty and filling in what I couldn't see. The room was still there, but not really. When I waved my hand, when I turned my head, there was nothing to be seen. My mother had gone blind, and my eyesight was already poor.

"You better go see the doctor," my friend said.

"I guess so," I replied.

Normally when I ring my doctor for an appointment, it is several days before the staff can fit me in. This time when I rang, the response was as per usual.

"We are fully booked until next week."

"Oh," I said. "Okay."

"Unless it's an emergency."

"Well," I said, "I'm not sure, but I seem to have no peripheral vision on the right side."

"Oh," said the receptionist. I could hear her typing. "We can see you at ten this morning."

I put down the phone and made coffee. Over the next hour, my peripheral vision on my right side began to return, until it had restored itself completely.

My mother died from aortic dissection. That is, the main artery that led from her heart disintegrated one day. She was with a friend when she collapsed in, of all places, a pharmacy. She was taken to hospital, where staff spent the day figuring out what was wrong with her, my sister Phyllis and her husband, Clyde, at her side. Because my other siblings and I had moved away, the large task of always being there as my parents grew older fell upon our sister Phyllis, and she rose to the challenge gracefully. Informed of the options, my mother decided against surgery, which would have entailed flying her to Vancouver and sawing her sternum open and spreading her ribs apart in order to repair the aorta, a procedure with a fairly low success rate for someone of eighty-five. She was comfortable and as with it as ever. The doctor said she could last a month, she could last a day, there was no way of telling. All her life my mother was prone to malapropisms, and this day, her last, was no different. When discussing her options, she said to Phyl and Clyde, "No erotics" when what she meant was "No heroics." Everyone in the room fell about laughing, including my mother.

And then, a few hours later, she died.

She was old, her heart was old, her aorta was worn out.

She'd suffered from heart palpitations—atrial fibrillation (which she always called fibulations, like tribulations, which of course they were)—for a number of years. She was blind, having lost the sight in both eyes to macular degeneration (first one eye, then, three years later, the other); she'd had to give up most of her favourite activities, including reading, quilting, watching hockey, and play-ing bridge. She still lived independently in her own place, but that winter had been very hard. She'd made the decision to move into sheltered accommodation—assisted living—which would have been an enormous wrench. So, as always, she had great timing, bowing out with minimal fuss, dropping dead, or near enough, which was something to which she had aspired.

But my siblings and I were not ready for her to leave us. We will never be ready.

When I think of my mother now, three and a half years after she died, my heart aches, it really does. This is not metaphorical. My heart aches, my throat tightens, and my eyes fill with tears. A physical response to a strange and abstract, unreal but of course completely real, state: my mother's absence from my life. My heart aches.

HISTORY OF PRESENT ILLNESS CONTINUED:
The wife is doing all the cooking, laundry, shopping, banking, has a homemaker once a week for heavy housekeeping. This man is on aspirin daily for stroke prevention, but I fear it may be too late given his frontal lobe features today. Certainly the caregiver stress and burden and the wife's ambivalence and need for absolution in letting this man go to facility care is one of the important considerations in this man's presentation.

PAST ILLNESSES:
Hypertension, smoked forty pack/year history, quit in 1983, longstanding peripheral vascular disease problems with aortofemoral bypass in 1983, recurrent UTIs with prostate surgery in 1988 for benign prostatic hypertrophy, fall in 1988 with fracture and recurrent fracture in 1993, both times general anesthetics, which he tolerated poorly. He had a double hernia and reverse colostomy after complications from his fractured hip in 1993 (fistula) for which he was given a spinal anesthetic. He had a blocked pancreatic duct, which is now diet controlled, bladder neck contracture in 1992, benign prostatic hypertrophy in 1988—surgery then and he now has a wound on his leg, which is being attended to by home care nursing.

MEDICATIONS
Adafat XL 30 mg once daily, ASA 160 mg daily, Sulfatrim DS for 8 days, Oxazepam 15 at hs, multivitamin, zinc, Docusate and Senokot.

ALLERGIES
Intolerant to general anesthetics, Morphine, Largactil, and Codeine all causing delirium.

Once I got to the doctor's surgery, I was seen quickly. The practice where we are registered is housed in a new building with plenty of natural light; it serves as a GP training centre as well. I've never seen the same doctor twice, but I don't mind; the GPs are always young and personable, better-looking than the cast of a hospital drama on TV. Who needs a family doctor when you can have a procession of good-looking thirty-year-olds all keen to prove themselves?

The doctor who saw me this time was very sweet and thorough; her entire face opened wide with excitement when I described my symptoms. She embarked on a range of simple tests—shining lights into my eyes, hitting my knee with a hammer—all of which I passed. I'd figured out by now that, whatever it was that had taken place, it was unlikely to indicate anything wrong with my eyes but was more likely to be neurological. This was not a relief. She consulted one of her more senior colleagues and decided that I probably hadn't had a stroke, but that I should be assessed for TIA, a Transient Ischemic Attack—not a stroke but stroke-like symptoms that may act as a stroke warning. I would need to attend the TIA clinic at hospital on Friday.

That night as I sat in front of the TV, I had another little episode: flashing lights in my right eye, accompanied by bars of distortion, faces distorting on the screen. This could, of course, have been psychosomatic; by now I was gripped by the idea that there was something wrong with my brain.

My friend, safely home in Vancouver, sent me a Jewish joke: an

Italian, a German, and Jew go for a walk. The Italian says, "I am so thirsty. I must have wine." The German says, "I am so thirsty. I must have beer." The Jew says, "I am so thirsty. I must have diabetes."

My parents married during the Second World War, and they were absolutely devoted to each other; they were each other's heart's content, their love for each other unswerving and not dimmed with time and age. My mother's elder sister, also called Phyllis, had made a bad marriage earlier on during the war; when her husband, Duncan, returned to BC from the European front, he brought with him several items of war booty, including a huge Nazi flag he had liberated in Holland and a Dutch girlfriend. He divorced Phyllis and married this other woman. Phyllis was devastated. She moved in with my parents, and not long after she died of a broken heart, or that's what people said—except in this case it was true: she died of heart failure caused by cardiac valve disease, which itself was probably caused by the rheumatic fever she had as a child, both conditions that, had she lived a few years more, were to become treatable.

Her heart was broken, and she died, and I know that this early death of her beloved sister caused my mother heartache for the rest of her life.

When you look at your child, sometimes you feel as though your heart will burst, with pride of course, but also with joy. *Look at him!* you think. *Look at her!* Miraculous, gorgeous, bigger than life, larger than the sex you had in order to conceive, greater than any other love, your giant, overpowering child. I look at my children and feel as though my heart will burst from all this love. And I cannot look away.

FUNCTIONAL INQUIRY:
He requires a great deal of assistance, prompting, directing and cueing because of his visuospatial

problems, which are likely vascular and fronto-temporal parietal in etiology. His wife is doing a lot in the way of self-care for the man and his basic activities of daily living because of incapacities. He has few pastimes, hobbies, and interests now owing to problems with vision and brain disease. He fabricates and his history is unreliable and he needs corroboration for all manner of testimony.

REVIEW OF SYSTEMS:
Unreliable. He has dentures that are ill fitting His appetite is good. His mood can be crabby at times. Primary caregiver not here to corroborate. Vision in his left eye is poor due to macular disease. He mobilizes with a cane and walker. Says he has a scooter. He feeds himself, helps her cook which is not true. He has been at the Saanich Peninsula before for respite and says he exercises there twice a day and he exercises at home which I seriously doubt.

The baby GP referred me to the TIA clinic. I've lived in Britain for a long time now, and I'm accustomed to listening to the British complain about their health service. But, apart from having babies, this was my first serious encounter with the NHS, and it performed like a well-oiled, albeit acronym-laden, machine. I found myself in front of an urbane neurologist called Henry.

"You look healthy," he said.

"I am healthy," I replied.

He set me up for a full battery of tests that afternoon, which turned out to be rather more sophisticated than hitting my knee with a rubber mallet. An ECG, or electrocardiogram, which measures the electrical activity of the heart, its rhythm and pace. Then a CT scan, or computerized tomography scan, created by a sophisticated X-ray machine that takes pictures of cross-sections, or slices, of the brain. Then a carotid artery ultrasound, a high-frequency radio scan that creates images of the two large arteries in the neck. And, finally, a series of blood tests.

They were looking at my heart to see if it was working properly, at my brain for evidence of stroke or bleeding, and at my major arteries in case they were clogged up or damaged in any way. They were looking for the things that killed my parents.

This is overly dramatic. It's not as though my parents' deaths were premature: he was eighty-four, she was eighty-five. We all have to die of something, whether it's a broken heart or furred-up arteries. The NHS was doing its bit to prevent this from happening to me anytime soon.

PHYSICAL EXAMINATION:
He is a well turned out, bright, alert eighty-three-year-old man, tall, with a degree of osteoporosis clinically. Examination of the vital signs: blood pressure 140/80 with no postural drop, pulse 76 and regular. Weight 81.2 kg, height 173 cm. Examination of the head and neck—ear canals are clear. Pupils are equal and reactive though he has bilateral macular disease in the right worse than the left, I thought. Nose and mouth—mild atrophic changes only. Ill-fitting dentures. No lymphadenopathy, thyroid abnormality, or carotid or vertebral bruit. Examination of the chest—air excursion normal, air entry equal bilaterally. Air excursion fair. No adventitious sounds. Examination of the cardiovascular system—peripheral pulses are diminished somewhat. No real swelling of ankles though it is hard to tell with one of the ankles wrapped because of skin disease that I did not look at today. Ulceration presumably. No signs of cardiac decompensation. Jugular venous pressure normal. Heart sounds normal. No murmurs, bruits,

or extra sounds. Examination of the abdomen—soft, non-tender, no guarding, rigidity, masses or organomegaly. No suprapubic abnormalities. Genital rectal examination deferred. Neurological examination—no obvious lateralizing features. Power, tone and reflexes all about equal symmetrically. He had trouble with the left capsulitis, so I couldn't test pronator drift. Plantar reflexes equivocal in the left, downgoing on the right. Tongue protrusion central. Frontal release signs positive.

MENTAL STATUS EXAMINATION
He scored 18/30. 6/10 on orientation with three more near misses. 3/3 on registration, 4/5 on attention and calculation for backward spelling. 3/5 with numbers. 0/3 on recall getting all three with simple prompting and 5/9 on language skills with real problems in following written instructions. Verbal instructions were also mildly but significantly impaired. He had true Gertmann's syndrome with left right confusion localized to the left angular gyrus.

My parents were famously devoted to each other. After my father died, when I was helping my mother sort through his things, she told me that his devotion had sometimes been a little hard to bear. "He always needs to know where I am, what I'm doing," she said. This became more oppressive as his physical and mental health failed. "But," she said, switching to the past tense, "his heart belonged to me. He loved me absolutely—he was never remotely interested in other women." And she was glad of that. In later years, his devotion to her meant he wasn't remotely interested in anyone apart from her, including his children; he'd become such a serious arteriopath that there wasn't room in his heart for anyone else but her.

I went back to hospital for an echocardiogram bubble test: an ultrasound examination of the heart conducted after a bubble of saline solution has been injected into the bloodstream, its progress visible on the ultrasound screen.

A couple of weeks had passed since my last set of hospital tests, and I'd had no further episodes of weird bits of my range of vision disappearing. So far, I had passed all the tests. I was becoming blasé, more interested in the anthropology of hospital workers and their sophisticated procedures than in my own results. I lay on my side on the gurney; the technician asked me to blow air into a paper bag in order to increase the pressure on my heart as the saline solution moved through my bloodstream and into my heart. He asked me to blow hard again, and again.

This time I failed the test. The echocardiogram bubble test revealed a hole in my heart.

DEPRESSION SCALE:
3/15, not elevated.

ASSESSMENT:
1. Probably frontal lobe disease likely vascular in etiology accounting for discrepancy between the dependency functionally and psychologically.
2. Arteriopathy, widespread hypertension, smoking related peripheral vascular disease with previous bypass surgeries twenty years ago.
3. Fractured hip 1988, refractured in 1993 affecting gait and balance. Has a shoe lift.
4. Urinary dysfunction likely local and central causes, may need to see the urologist for recurrent contracture.
5. Caregiver stress.

The human heart has two sides—left ventricle and right ventricle—separated by a wall. Blood should not pass through this wall. When we are in the womb, a small flap in the wall allows oxygenated blood to pass from one ventricle to the other. When we are born, this flap closes permanently as we take our first breath.

Or at least it should. In around 20 per cent of the population, the flap does not close, allowing venous blood—the blood that's travelled around your body already and is now depleted of oxygen and possibly contains debris picked up along the way—to pass from one side of the heart to the other. As is the case with me.

Most people with patent foramen ovale, or PFO—at last, an acronym to call my own!—live long, healthy lives entirely unaware that they have a hole in their heart.

I returned to Henry with the result.

"Okay," he said.

"Okay," I replied.

"I'm going to order an MRI. We'll take a good look, in case there's any buildup of debris in your brain."

When I was a teenager, I lived with my parents on a hill above a lagoon on the West Coast. My siblings are a fair bit older than I am, and by the time we moved to this house, they had long since left home, got married, and had babies. The beach that ran along the spit of land that formed the lagoon was like all beaches in the Pacific Northwest, the high tide line cluttered with driftwood and seaweed. Debris. This was what I pictured as I talked to Henry.

The MRI did not take place at the hospital with which I had become so cosily familiar. Instead the NHS farmed me out to a private clinic in Golder's Green. I took the tube to get there, giving myself plenty of time to find it. The clinic was slick and glossy, like a place that could give you Botox along with your brain scan. To get to the examination room, I walked through a dark corridor where technicians sat in front of banks of computers; through the observation windows were the scanners—huge white machines, like undersea submersibles. The technician strapped me in and told me to expect "loud and prolonged bursts of alarming noise." He asked me to choose a radio station. I picked the familiar chatter of BBC Radio 4. He tightened my head straps and left the room.

"Loud and prolonged bursts of alarming noise" was an understatement. The MRI made a sound like the heaviest of heavy metal bands testing the amps at the biggest stadium gig of all time. Brain scan meets Spinal Tap. God only knows what an actual spinal tap sounds like. The Radio 4 lunchtime news didn't stand a chance.

> PLAN
> I am not aware of any medications that will help this man nor am I aware of any rehabilitation that could help him either. I am dubious that there is a great deal more I can offer this man beyond these comments. I don't think he needs antidepressants. I don't think memory drugs will do much good with a story like this. I think the family and wife in particular need absolution to move this man to placement in a fairly immediate time frame.

My father was sick for twenty-five years, a wheelchair-bound invalid for the last fifteen years of his life. The forty-cigarettes-a-day habit he picked up when he was a teenager had resulted in an array of symptoms and difficulties. In the early years of his deterioration, each time I went to visit I was sure I'd never see him alive again, but then I got used to it. My siblings and I all got used to it, and it felt as though he'd probably live forever in his grumpy, demanding, hard-to-be-with kind of way.

My mother cared for him, year after year, and this care took a large toll on her own health. Only occasionally could she be persuaded to take a break, coming to visit me in London, my brother in the Okanagan, or my other sister in Nova Scotia. During one of these breaks Phyllis took my father in for a neurological consultation; in his report the consultant gives my mother "absolution." If science is our religion, doctors are our work-a-day priests. This report enabled my mother to relinquish my father's care to other people. He did not go into sheltered accommodation but straight into long-term extended care in a hospital, such was his condition. We were told that, in caring for him on her own at home, our mother had been doing the work of five nurses.

The MRI scan showed that my brain is entirely healthy. No sign of scarring or damage from debris, driftwood, or seaweed.

I had a final session with Henry.

"New research is showing a link between PFO and migraine," he said. "It's early days. Your symptoms could have been caused by migraine—migraine aura, effectively."

"Oh," I said. "Okay." I did have a headache at the time, but I would not have described it as a "migraine"—I've never suffered from anything that I would describe as a "migraine." I took Henry's explanation to mean the following: we don't really know what happened to you that morning. As far as we can see, you are perfectly healthy.

"So," I said. "PFO. Anything else I should know about it?"

Henry shook his head, almost ruefully. "No. Most people live with it without ever knowing about it."

"Okay," I said. "Well, thank you."

"Oh," said Henry, "there is one thing. You're not a scuba diver, are you?"

"No," I said, as I pictured the MRI submersible safe in its north London clinic.

"Don't take it up. PFO hearts can't take the pressure—that hole will leak more or possibly get bigger."

"Okay," I said. "Thanks."

We shook hands, and I left the hospital for the final time, better informed but none the wiser.

My siblings and I are all getting older, and our parents are both gone. But we carry them with us in our hearts as well as in our genes. We carry them with us always.

THIS DOCUMENT HAS BEEN DICTATED AND ACCEPTED
by Dr.————,
CONSULTATION
07/Mar/2001/ @ 1715

BAD Back

Richard Steel

As the first, and only, son of an English father and Canadian mother, I grew up in London, England. From an early age I was aware that backs should be strong, shoulders broad, spines straight and true, capable of carrying the emotional and physical burdens of the world. Sports teams ideally had a strong backbone, which could lead to victory despite some weaker extremities on the team. The comics I read as a boy in the 1960s largely involved the British Army in the Second World War and were full of sergeant-majorly admonishments to "Put your back into it, you spineless shower of nancy boys!" and pictures of row after row of ramrod-straight backs on the parade ground.

It's not just the army. "And so we must straighten our backs and work for our freedom," said Martin Luther King Jr. "A man can't ride you unless your back is bent." The implication is clear: without a straight and strong spine, a man will be submissive and unworthy of respect. Not a real man. This attitude was reinforced at school.

My father had been through that same war and seen his brother killed early on in the conflict. He was a traditional man who had great internal strength and determination. As he had done, so did I. My trunk was loaded with a tartan (McLeod, if I remember rightly) dressing gown, slippers, singlets, forty-eight handkerchiefs, a few thousand of my mother's tears, and along with it, I was packed off to "prep" school. All clothing needed printed labels sewn in appropriate places. My mother hated sewing and loved modern, labour-saving inventions, so the Ronco Buttoneer soon labelled all my clothes with little plastic studs instead of thread. The studs were as scratchy as hell, and my ankles, neck, and lower back were constantly irritated, bearing the scars of progress.

The school was a boys' only boarding school in Broadstairs, Kent, southeast England. The building itself was a huge Gothic edifice. There were turrets full of bats, rows of rattling twelve-by-four-foot single-pane sash windows, worn tiled floors, hollowed-out concrete steps, pull-chain toilet cisterns, and greaseproof toilet paper. A veritable *Hammer House of Horror*. (In his wisdom, Charles Dickens chose to set *Bleak House* in Broadstairs.)

There was no heating in the dormitories: thirty boys, in two rows beneath thirty-foot-high vaulted ceilings, as cold as the North Pole. Heavy cast-iron bedsteads, horsehair mattresses, not enough blankets (more horsehair), and lumpy pillows. To me, however, my bed was sanctuary, a surrogate home where I could be alone, away from everything and everyone, where I could dream of smiles and warmth and half-term holidays. It was as if I could lift up the blankets and rays of light and warmth would welcome me in. These reveries would be shattered from time to time by an invasion from one or more of my fellow dormitory dwellers, flicking wet towels at my arms and legs as I tried to protect the more sensitive parts of my body. I would stay in bed in the mornings until the very last second, hanging on to my alternative world, risking tardiness for chapel and a consequent slippering.

We wore shorts (horsehair again, or so they felt) year-round. In those days we would get cold winters and considerable snowfall. I had two years of raw, red, chapped thighs that hurt so much I cried. Once you made it to a school prefect, you could wear trousers, but I never made it, as the school closed down through lack of funds. Not enough people wanted to go there.

All this barbarism was supposed to make men of us small boys, to teach us to be humble and to suffer adversity but come out strong little men, with broad shoulders, straight spines, and stiff upper lips.

The spine physically supports the casing of the brain and is the channel of all movement and feeling in the body. Thirty-three vertebrae in five sections, from the larger, lower lumbars to the higher, more delicate cervical vertebrae of the neck: an incredibly designed network of bone, cartilage, and nerves offering support, protection, and the mechanics for all upper-body movement. The backbone is "behind" every organ in the body, so you could say it is "behind" every thought, and every heartbeat.

But I have a "bad back." Sometimes my back "goes" or "has gone," as in "Aaargh! My back's just gone!" I occasionally get headaches, but I don't say I have a bad head. I am more frequently affected by bouts of bursitis, tendonitis, and maybe arthritis, but my elbow never "goes," my ankle is "stiff" or "sore" but still attached to me. These descriptions contain some hope, or at least the chance of the condition being corrected, whereas, for as long as I can remember having problems with my back, I have labelled it as *bad* or *gone*, something to be dismissed as so catastrophic and chronic that it is to be scolded and jettisoned from the rest of me.

It infuriates me. Invariably I am temporarily crippled by it just as I need to be active. Maybe I can't accept its weakness and how that reflects on me. I'm not sure about that, but I do know that my relationship to my back is at the core of my being, and that the implication of a bad back is that I am providing my brain and heart (among other organs) with a feeble support mechanism . . . All of this leaves me feeling compromised and even inadequate in ways beyond back pain and the inability to fulfill the demands of a splenetic sergeant major.

In *The Descent of Man*, Charles Darwin suggested that the time when our ancestors first became bipedal was the most important developmental factor in our species getting to where we are now. By walking on two feet, with an increasingly strong and straight spine, we freed our hands, which in turn advanced our minds as we learned to make and use tools.

There seems to be some confusion as to when this happened, either with the *Orrorin tugenensis* of what is now Kenya, six million years ago, or the more recent *Australopithecus anamensis* at four million years ago. Either way, those first steps were a very long time ago, certainly long enough to hope that the transformation should be successfully completed by now. Unfortunately not quite, in my case.

What's really happening to me physically has never been completely clear. It has been described to me in different ways, by different people, and unfailingly, perhaps deliberately, I never retain much of what I'm told. It seems, however, to be something along these lines: I have some kind of congenital abnormality, sometimes described as a congenital weakness, at a specific point in the lumbar region of my spine. This has led to a spondylolisthesis ("slipped disc") of my L5 vertebra. Not a big deal on its own, I just have a bit more fluidity than is ideal in that area. A few discs in the lumbar section are slightly compressed, and one disc is bulging. This is largely wear and tear, and, again, on its own has no great effect on anything. There is a nice little scoliosis (sideways curve to the spine) in there somewhere, a bit higher up. This could have occurred at birth, but I've never been sure. There are also a few outcrops of osteophytes here and there, proudly growing like coral reefs, waiting to irritate any nerve that happens to swim too close.

These ingredients on their own are to some extent fairly benign, but shaken up together they synergize into a particularly potent and bitter cocktail: "The Spasm," perhaps.

The bigger and more complex problem, however, is probably the overworking and compensating that the muscles in my feet, legs, hips, buttocks, and back have been doing for most, if not all, of my life. In trying to correct or protect me from the implications of any congenital imbalance, these muscles have created imbalances of their own. This can make treatment particularly complicated and frustrating. An improvement in one area can lead to a crisis in another, as underused muscles are suddenly called into action and overused muscles are asked to work even harder.

Two years ago I signed up with a physiotherapist with whom I felt very comfortable. He focused mainly on my hips and buttocks, and as well as exercises and some laying on of hands, he practised the "Gunn technique," which is a method of a rapid insertion of an acupuncture needle into a particularly tense muscle. A sharp pain would ensue as the tension literally exploded, usually resulting in a tide of relief. After a few weeks, I felt real progress with my back, less pain, and a greater freedom of movement. Unfortunately, this improvement was accompanied by a ruptured abdominal muscle, along with a constant pain, and strain, in my hips and groin. For three months I could hardly walk, so I stopped going to him, and stopped those exercises, and within a week I could walk more freely. Naturally my back immediately regressed, and we returned to square one.

There seem to be so many combinations of causes and effects, involving muscles, vertebrae, discs, and joints, that I now have no clue where pains originate and for what reason.

I can't remember exactly—probably due to my mind being inadequately supported—but I would guess that for the last eight years I have not had a day when I have been free from pain or, at least, discomfort. My hip and leg muscles ache; I have a band of mild pain across my lower back, and a tired and groaning middle back. Then there are the occasional, if I'm lucky, "events" when my back "goes."

These can, and usually do, happen in seemingly innocuous circumstances, often within an hour of waking, before I have all my defences in place. Sneezing, putting on a shoe, waving, stroking the cat, almost anything will do the trick. If I go to lift something, or do some strenuous activity, my abdominal muscles and back muscles are tensed and supportive, but I am not prepared for sneezing. These minor actions are usually preceded by a long drive, airplane travel, sitting in a theatre, raking leaves, digging, or working more than a bare minimum in the preceding days. The event itself is merely the final straw. They vary in intensity and seem to have an epicentre in the middle of my lower back or in a few other specific points across my sacrum. With no warning I will feel a stiletto (the knife, not the heel, although the latter might be more enjoyable) pierce deep and true and open me up leaving a precise, red gash and a feeling of total vulnerability. If you imagine a fig sliced open by a razor blade, then that is how I see the feeling. The pain is dramatic, rapid, and searing, causing my eyes to pop and water and my body to freeze to prevent the pain stabbing again.

Then follows an agonized collection of hot-water bottles, ice packs, arnica, Advil, and the hunched and twisted retreat to the floor or bed, to be flat and totally immobile. And there I'll stay for one day, two days, anywhere up to ten. At the time of an event I feel I instantly age twenty-five years, walking or, rather, shuffling just like my father in his final years. I have witnessed too much decay and immobility in the time leading up to the deaths of both my parents, a few aunts, my godmother, some friends, and a couple of people I "buddied" to the end of their lives. I have no patience left for it; I don't want to see any more, and I certainly don't want to see it in me.

This fear and my training at school could be the reasons why I have an almost unnatural ability to sleep in times of stress or when my back deserts me. I shut down: I don't think, I don't move. Hours can stretch into days if necessary. I dream, emerging on occasion to test my mental and physical strengths, but usually retreat to try again twelve hours later. I know that it is recommended that one should keep moving after your back has "gone." My sojourns are particular to me: to get me through the initial crisis until I can summon some mental and physical hope again. I hide in bed so I don't have to be in the midst of my family, being old, grumpy, and useless, someone to be humoured, to be pitied.

The first time my back misbehaved I was at my second, more solvent, "prep" school. This one was closer to home, and not quite so Dickensian, although it did have its odd, sadistic rituals to keep us boys in our places. A much-treasured prize was a traditionally styled green wool cap, which was handed out to those who had played consistently well in various sports for the school teams. Not many of these were awarded, but when they were the whole school would gather around the twelve-foot-long, full-height outside urinal to howl as the prized cap was tossed over a wall to land in the orange-stained trough and then to jeer as the boy being honoured fished it out, dripping and stinking. An unusual form of celebration.

A while before I was awarded my cap, on the eve of an important soccer game against a rival school, I felt my lower back lock on my left side. There was no great pain, but I could hardly walk, let alone run. I informed the games master, who didn't like what he heard and sent me to the nurse. She looked, prodded, bent me over, and declared there was nothing wrong with me. I insisted I couldn't walk but didn't have the vocabulary to explain further. I was labelled "spineless," and the award of my green cap was delayed until I had made amends.

Now, after years of physical therapies and much thinking and analyzing of the nuances of how my back works and feels, I have a far more extensive vocabulary, although I suspect it wouldn't have got me any more sympathy had I compared my back to a fig.

After that, nothing, as I went through my teens and twenties, apart from poor posture and a tiredness in my middle back. Then, *wham!* I'm thirty-six years old and getting out of the bath with our one-year-old daughter in my arms. The first stiletto stab and suddenly I'm sweating, dribbling, and talking just like a one-year-old. My eyes wild and body twisted, clutching our daughter. Since that bath, my back has "gone" increasingly frequently. For the last eight months I have had an event every two to three weeks.

I have learned to listen and feel the moods of my body, and to respond accordingly. I have practised the Alexander Technique, had regular acupuncture, visited a chiropractor for a number of years, consulted surgeons and specialists, returned frequently to my family doctor, attended a wonderful osteopath, who also happens to be my sister, and been treated by a number of different physiotherapists.

I hang upside down on an inversion table, practise yoga; I have tried Pilates and follow a daily exercise and stretching program. I suspect I would be worse off without all this, but it is depressing to be no better. A couple of years ago, I decided to stop all treatments as I found myself being pulled in so many different directions, like a cheap cut of meat, being prepared and tenderized, albeit very skilfully and sympathetically. All these treatments and exercises can feed perhaps the biggest fear of my condition: that I become solely a "bad back," with everything I do being related to it and all relationships based on it.

Now, as I walk down the street, I am greeted with inquiries into the condition of my back often before I am greeted by name. My family will ask, "How's your back?" upon my waking or if they haven't seen me for a few hours. They mean well, but it saddens me that before being recognized as a husband, father, genius, the condition of my back looms larger. This is in no way a criticism but is an example of how much the state of my back affects our lives and how desperate that can make me feel.

But here's the rub. I know that 80 per cent of men and women in the industrialized world older than forty-five years of age suffer from some form of back pain, chronic or occasional. In 1994, the direct and indirect costs of back and spine disorders in Canada alone exceeded $8.1 billion.

So it's common as muck! Not exceptional at all, just another case of the human body not yet adapting to the rigours of a modern world. Bad backs being so common, I get a lot of advice and recommendations for treatments and get to hear other people's stories. "What you need to do every morning is rub a mixture of horseradish, garlic, and lemon juice into your lower back. I've never had a day's trouble since." That kind of thing. My back and its bad behaviour has become public property.

Enough. I am fortunate that my bad back is not a terminal condition, and I have not had to undergo any toxic treatments or suffer nearly as much pain as others. I generally feel myself to be a very lucky person, though at times that luck can feel fragile—and at times I even feel absurdly guilty, as if the whole thing was somehow my fault. I know this is ridiculous: my wicked back originates from a congenital weakness or abnormality; it's just the roll of the dice or the result of some stress (the main cause of back trauma) at or around the time of my birth.

However, I am certainly not going to blame my mother, who had a horrific-enough time giving birth to me. My parents were in New York at that time, and as my mother entered labour, my father took her to the designated hospital in Manhattan. She was in pain and did not keep it to herself. The staff told her to calm down and be quiet (stop being so spineless?), but she could not, or would not. Consequently, they strapped her wrists and her ankles to the trolley she was lying on, and then left her, alone, in a corridor, in the basement to cool off. Perhaps this was standard procedure in 1960 in New York, but I can't see this being for her, or even my, benefit.

An hour after my birth, delighted to have a son, my father sent a telegram across the Atlantic addressed to: The Headmaster, Haversham House Preparatory School for Boys, Broadstairs, Kent, England . . . Just the mention of the place sends a shiver down my spine. I'd better go and lie down.

kidney, pancreas . . .

The Frankenstein Syndrome, or Giving Away the Body

Stephen Gauer

> It was already one in the morning; the rain pattered dismally against the panes, and my candle was nearly burnt out, when, by the glimmer of the half-extinguished light, I saw the dull yellow eye of the creature open; it breathed hard, and a convulsive motion agitated its limbs.
>
> ——Mary Shelley, *Frankenstein*

In the field of medical anthropology, the phrase *Frankenstein syndrome* refers to the irrational belief on the part of an organ donor, or an organ donor's family, that the donated organ carries into its new human home the particular qualities, quirks, and personality traits of the donor. If I'm a kind, generous person and give my heart, lungs, or kidneys to another person, for example, then these positive qualities will carry over as well. The phrase refers to the 1931 Hollywood film, based on an earlier stage version of the Mary Shelley novel. In the film (unlike in the novel), Herr Frankenstein unknowingly implants a criminal's brain in the skull of his creation; this is suggested as the reason for the creature's violent, homicidal behaviour. This literal causality, criminal brain equals monstrous killer, is simple and obvious enough for a child to comprehend; indeed, *Frankenstein* is the first film that truly and completely terrified me. I have a very clear memory of watching it on TV late on a Sunday afternoon in May. I was eight years old and spent a good part of that sleepless night hiding under the blankets in my bed.

I am thinking about transplanted brains and Victor Frankenstein and his syndrome because in a very small way he is part of my story, and I need to understand more clearly the power and revulsion his name evokes. In 2007, when I was fifty-five years old, I donated my left kidney to my granddaughter Amelia, who was suffering from a rare disease, Henoch-Schönlein purpura, that had been systematically attacking her kidney function for ten years. She'd already had one transplant, in 1997, when she was sixteen, from a dead donor. Now she needed another. The waiting list was too long, at six to eight years, and the alternative treatment, three dialysis treatments a week, four hours each, was too painful and exhausting. She needed a live donor. I was a blood match and fit enough to donate, so I gave her a kidney. Amelia is not my biological granddaughter, and so a mocking, unconscious version of the Frankenstein syndrome kicked in immediately and effortlessly. I joked that the Gauer kidney was smart, well read, and preferred the Beatles to the Rolling Stones. I joked that the Gauer kidney was used to an excellent and healthy diet, no fast food and plenty of veggies, and that therefore Amelia must curb her desire for pizza and popcorn. I joked that the Gauer kidney, being of German construction, was extremely well made and therefore likely to last a long time. Sadly, this prediction proved to be untrue, because Amelia died less than a year after the transplant.

When we donate an organ, are we giving away more than human tissue? Why are we so ambivalent and conflicted about making the decision to donate, on the one hand, and yet so sentimental in praising donors, on the other? Where is the reasonable middle ground between Frankenstein paranoia and gooey "gift of life" rhetoric that turns donors into saints? These are useful if difficult questions to pose about organ donation, and in trying to answer them, medical anthropologists who study organ donation have built up an impressive body of analysis and commentary. They talk about the "commodification of the body"—how a human body can now be broken down into one hundred and fifty useful components for sale on the open market, fetching more than two hundred and fifty thousand dollars in total. The anthropologists attack, with justifiable outrage, the illegal trade in human organs that typically sees a poor single male in Rio de Janeiro, Manila, or Calcutta sell a kidney for one thousand dollars to a wealthy American, Israeli, or European. They describe the twin deaths of brain-dead donors—once when the brain dies and again when the organs are removed. They track with great precision the complicated dynamics of donation, focusing on conflict and disagreement. Family members feel pressured to donate. Sons resent donating to domineering mothers. Donors are shunned when recipients die. Recipients feel overbearing gratitude that makes donors uncomfortable. Strangers donate to strangers to meet their own needs of approval, accomplishment, or meaning.

My experience was far simpler. When neither Amelia's mother, Alison, nor her grandmother, Judith (my partner), were able to donate, I was the logical next choice, a healthy man in his mid-fifties with no children of his own. I knew that Amelia was unlikely to live a long life, but my spending a week in hospital followed by a couple of weeks of recovery, in all a month of idleness and discomfort, seemed a reasonable exchange for possible better health and happiness for Amelia. I'd known Amelia since she was two, watched her grow into a young girl, teenager, and young woman. She was intensely likable, smart, funny, generous, a mix of girlish enthusiasms and pragmatic career goals ("I don't want to work with people," she told me once. "Pushing paper in a government office—that's the perfect job for me."). During the fifteen years Judith and I lived in Vancouver, Amelia came out regularly from Toronto for visits, accompanied by various passions of the moment: rollerblades, plush animals, the violin, Buffy the Vampire Slayer videos, the novels of John Grisham.

Self-interest can be a complicated knot to untie. After we moved back to Toronto in 2006, Amelia's illness was a difficult responsibility for my partner Judith (a retired nurse); every time the phone rang, Judith and I looked at each other and wondered if it was yet another call from Amelia or from the hospital saying she'd been admitted again. If necessary, Judith would wrangle the nurses and doctors in the emergency ward to make sure Amelia got the care she deserved. A transplant would stop that stressful cycle and make everyone's life, including mine, much easier. I realized again that I like a certain amount of risk and adventure in my life. The emotional geography of middle age is often flat and featureless. Why not take a chance and experience something new, and in the process learn something about myself? And I have to admit that throughout my life, rather like a small child, I have often sought the spotlight and enjoyed receiving praise for my actions. Some of these actions are easier to accomplish at twenty than at fifty-five.

My risk of dying during the transplant was less than three in ten thousand, but these numbers meant nothing. If the risk had been one in a hundred I still would have jumped. For five years in Vancouver, I sailed a small sloop single-handed in the Strait of Georgia, all year long, in good weather and bad. Every time I left the dock, knowing I was heading out alone on the ocean, I felt a frisson of nervous excitement. Every time my feet touched the dock again, I felt an intense sense of safe arrival and accomplishment. At various times of my life, I've hitchhiked alone across North America and Europe, driven a motorcycle through Texas thunderstorms, slept in orange groves in Algeria and Tunisia, trekked in Nepal, dropped acid and shot speed, had unprotected sex with a prostitute, been groped by gay truck drivers, and painted houses while balancing on tall ladders. I've enjoyed other types of risks too. I've been penniless, worked freelance, run a business, and shuffled jobs like cards in a deck. In love, I've been sometimes reckless and impulsive. Once, in my twenties, working at a newspaper in Manitoba, I had an affair with a woman married to a hard rock miner named James, a violent man skilled with dynamite who claimed the union had a vendetta against him and wanted him dead. James had already left Pat and gone back to Quebec when I started sleeping with her, but he came back to town unexpectedly one weekend. I ran into them at a shopping mall. Pat performed the introductions. I was convinced James knew about us and would pull out a gun at any moment and shoot me. Instead, he smiled and slapped me on the back. As they walked away, I felt, I am ashamed to say, an almost overwhelming sense of masculine victory.

The prospect of major surgery did not scare me. On the morning of the operation, June 26, 2007, I felt intensely alive, like the moment at the top of the ladder, or pushing off from the dock, or surviving the Texas rainstorm. For five months the intense emotions surrounding the transplant and the anticipation of how it might change our lives had filled my heart to overflowing. If at that moment someone had turned and asked me why I was there, I would have burst into tears. There were fifteen of us waiting in the admissions office at Toronto General Hospital, all middle-aged or older. A young clerk took our health cards and then called us in twos and threes, and another clerk led us to a yet another waiting room. Then my name was called. I changed into a hospital gown and put blue cloth booties on my bare feet. I handed my bag to someone and walked to the prep room, a large open space holding about twenty beds, and got up onto a bed.

A nurse brought me a warm blanket. "How are you this morning?" she asked.

"Actually," I said, "I feel very excited."

She smiled. "Oh," she said. "That's a bit different."

How could I even begin to explain what I was feeling? Lines from a Theodore Roethke poem kept running through my mind.

> I wake to sleep and take my waking slow
> I feel my fate in what I cannot fear.

More people showed up to check how I was feeling, to ask me questions about allergies, and to reassure me that everything would be fine. They left. I lay there comfortably under the hot blanket.

The lines of poetry ran through my head again. Suddenly I was in motion. The clock on the wall said two minutes to eight, and there was no time to waste. They wheeled me down one hall, around a corner, and down the next hall. A fierce headwind was blowing in my face. Then a door opened and I was in an operating room lit brilliantly by a constellation of overhead lights. A nurse appeared on the right and helped me move from the gurney to a narrow table covered with a turquoise foam pad. A man standing to my left, the anesthesiologist, put an IV into my left arm. He asked me if I was comfortable and I said yes and we talked. Suddenly, with no warning, no countdown from one hundred, everything went black.

The kidney is one of the homelier organs, famous for its shape (like a pool or a bean) and for the fact that the human body has two but can function perfectly well with just one. In traditional Chinese medicine, the kidneys represent yin and yang and therefore should not be split up (the Torah claims, more menacingly, that the kidney on the right side prompts us to do good, whereas the kidney on the left side prompts us to do evil). The average kidney is four inches long and an inch and a half wide, weighs just five ounces, and has a colour somewhere between brown and blood red. You can easily hold two of them in one hand. What you're holding is an intricate filter that removes urea and dozens of other impurities and poisons from hundreds of litres of blood every day. The blood arrives from the aorta via the renal artery and returns to the body via the renal vein. The ureter takes urine to the bladder. The plumbing is simple and straightforward. But the kidney does more. It maintains the pH level of the body; regulates electrolytes, blood pressure, and blood volume; and produces important hormones such as urodilatin and renin and vitamin D. That's why dialysis is a poor substitute for a kidney; it provides only the mechanical equivalent of the kidney's filter and not its complex chemistry set.

My kidneys looked lovely the first time I saw them. I had gone for a CT scan at the hospital, one of dozens of tests required before I was given the okay for the transplant operation. The CT scan creates an enormous 3-D image of the kidneys. For this test, you lie down on a white bed in front of a huge, grey, doughnut-shaped machine. The technician inserts an IV into your left arm. A woman's voice coming from a speaker in the ceiling tells you to close your eyes and hold your breath. For a test run, the bed moves through the doughnut and back out again. If you peek, you see a sign overhead that says, "Close your eyes or the laser beam will blind you." The technician activates the IV. A liquid dye, used to improve the contrast of the image, enters your body. You feel a surge of heat flow through your body from head to foot. Then you feel like you've peed your pants. A funny metallic taste fills your mouth. None of these sensations inspires confidence. The bed moves into the doughnut and stops. You count to fifty. Then the bed pulls back out again. The technician removes the IV. The test is over. Later, the surgeon who was to perform the transplant showed me the image. There on the computer screen, rotating merrily in 3-D glory, were my two kidneys, purplish and plump, like distended fruit suspended from arteries branching from the skinny white aorta, the main blood vessel leading from the heart. My kidneys looked beautiful. The surgeon smiled.

Another day I ran a treadmill for fourteen minutes, boosted my pulse to 165, and then posed for an ultrasound. Afterward I saw something miraculous on the technician's video screen: the internal chambers of my own beating heart, the mitral valves flopping up and down like overexcited minnows. I had never looked into my body this way before. In a way it was like watching the Apollo astronauts walk on the moon. The images were eerily surreal, remote, fantastical, and utterly compelling.

But my experience was an aberration. For the most part we're more comfortable staring out into space than into our own bodies. Beyond the basics of anatomy, we know little about our insides. I have a better understanding of how the Internet works than how my own body works. I know the names of more parts of a sailboat than parts of my own body. I am wilfully ignorant of my own physical being, and it's not enough to blame Descartes, who separated mind from body, the traditions of Western philosophy, or anything else. I'm not sure we want to know more about what goes on beneath the skin.

The medical anthropologists cite our alienation from and objectification of the body as one of the reasons for the modern organ trade, legal and illegal, that affects nearly every nation on the planet. In *Strange Harvest: Organ Transplants, Denatured Bodies, and the Transformed Self*, Lesley Sharp explores such attitudes. "Increasingly, organs are thought of as just 'organs,'" writes Sharp, an anthropologist at Columbia's Barnard College in New York City, "rather than as living parts of a person that might be given willingly and unselfishly to others . . . this biological reductionism has insidious implications for constructions of self, definitions of what it means to be human, and more generally of life as it should be lived."

But the body is a machine, in a way, and we do tamper with its parts. We replace teeth and joints as easily as we do batteries in the remote. We mix aluminum, plastic, and steel with blood and muscle and tissue and never give it a moment's thought. The integrity of the body is a very loose and subjective concept. I gave away a kidney, but I feel no physical change, no lack or void. In a way, I'm proud that I allowed the kidney to be cut out of my body and placed into Amelia's body (looking at the video of the operation, all I can see are blue gowns and sheets; a small rectangle of pale, middle-aged flesh; an incision; clamps; metal instruments moving in and out; and the unsightly layers of muscle and fat visible just below the surface of my abdomen). Does the kidney belong to me? Of course. Is it mine to donate, to give away, even to sell? Yes. My body, myself.

When I came to after the operation, around noon, on the sixth floor of the acute care unit, I was connected to an IV line (via my wrist) and a catheter (via my penis to my bladder), and I had a nasal clip for oxygen. I felt fine. I felt better than fine. Thanks to the morphine I felt, well . . . euphoric. But once the morphine wore off, later that day, I didn't feel quite so wonderful. The incision hurt, and the bed wasn't comfortable no matter how I adjusted it. My throat was sore from the breathing tube used during the operation. I couldn't eat or drink. I had to sip tiny chunks of ice in a plastic cup. Every four hours, day and night, a nurse came and took my blood pressure and temperature. I had a button for dispensing morphine into the IV feed. This set-up is called a PCA (patient controlled analgesic) and means the patient has complete control over pain management, in theory at least. But pressing it didn't seem to make a huge difference.

On day two, the gas began. It is a function of the fact that the lower digestive tract does not like surgery and therefore shuts down. The gas got worse and worse. My belly swelled because gas is produced but not allowed to exit the body. Coughing and laughing caused acute pain. You must walk to relieve the gas, even though walking is painful and when you walk you shuffle down the hall like a tired old man. You have raced ahead in time. You are one hundred years old. On day three, at precisely 11:03 AM, I farted. This was good news for everyone. Violet, the day nurse, smiled and said I would be allowed to eat. Eating? What was that? I couldn't remember. She removed the IV line taped to my left wrist. This was good.

I went to see Amelia, who had her own room one floor up. She looked wonderful. She was sitting up in bed, a big smile on her face. "I feel eight thousand per cent better," she said. "How are you?"

"Oh," I said, "bad gas, very bad gas."

"Yeah, I know," she said. "I get that too sometimes."

The gas passed eventually. I ate a bit of food and read my books. I was bored and ready to leave. On Friday morning, the fourth day, I got up and walked down to the lobby of the hospital and bought two newspapers. I came back to the room and tried sitting in the chair. It didn't feel too bad. I got up and packed my bag. Judith arrived around noon. I got up again and put on my comfy yoga clothes and said goodbye to the nurses. When we walked out through the hospital door back into the world, the first thing I felt was the warm June sun on my face. How lovely that was. I took a deep breath. The air was stinky. I loved it. The traffic on University Avenue was noisier than I remembered. I loved that too.

I spent two weeks at home recovering. Mostly I sat on the front porch reading novels and watching the neighbours come and go. I felt like James Stewart in *Rear Window*, although there were no murders to observe. I couldn't drive or lift anything heavy. My body was still sore, especially the midsection. I had to carefully ease into and back out of a chair, or the bed, or the passenger seat of the car. I moved slowly not because I wanted to, but because I had no choice in the matter.

Three weeks after surgery, I went back to work as technical writer for one of the big banks. Downtown Toronto seemed noisier and more crowded than I remembered. I worked shorter days than usual; I found I was tired by three and so I'd go home. But by the end of the week, something had changed. One morning I got off the streetcar at Queen and Yonge and walked down to Front Street, as I always did, and for the first time since the operation I had no consciousness of my body. I was thinking about music and work and what I would eat for lunch. I looked at the crowds of people rushing to work and felt no different from them. And then I realized, this is how you recover, and this is when you know you're going to be all right.

In the July 27, 2009, issue of *The New Yorker*, a United Methodist pastor in Maryland named Kimberly Brown-Whale, fifty-three years old, described why she gave a kidney to a stranger, a middle-aged man from Rhode Island. "We can do more than we think we can," she said. "If you're sitting around with a good kidney you're not using, why can't someone else have it? For a couple of days of discomfort, someone else is freed from dialysis and able to live a full life. Gosh, I've had flus that made me feel worse."

Brown-Whale also talked about the concreteness of donating, how the action seemed more significant than the words she spoke in her church, the advice she gave to friends, the help she offered to members of her community. I would never donate to a stranger, but I understand her ground-level sense of generosity and matter-of-fact approach to donating. I made the decision to donate in a matter of minutes, while Judith had gone away for the weekend to visit a friend. At first I imagined having a series of serious discussions with myself all through Saturday and Sunday, weighing the pros and cons carefully, perhaps talking to friends and relatives to get their opinions and advice. But in fact, once Judith had left, I spent all of five minutes thinking about Amelia, my body, the kidney, the future, and immediately, perhaps impulsively, I posed the question, "Why not?" The question was not whether I would do it. The question was why would I not do it.

I knew I was healthy. I knew I didn't need two kidneys. But above all, I loved the clarity, for once in my life, of doing something absolutely good and useful for another human being, in this case a young woman in my family. Not my birth family, but my family of choice (when I announced my decision to donate, one birth family member surprised me by asking why Amelia didn't go to India for a kidney). The knot of self-interest would always be there, yes, but so would the jokes about the Gauer kidney. Our relationship did not fracture or slide sideways; in fact, Amelia and I grew closer after the operation. On the day she died, I was on my way to finish painting her apartment. She was finally moving out of her mother's house and into her own life. "Let me help you," I would say. And she would answer, "You are kind, Stephen, and I really really appreciate it."

Amelia died sometime during the night of April 5, 2008, exactly 284 days after the transplant. A week later, we gathered in a large meeting room at the University of Toronto to celebrate her life. When Alison, her mother, stood up to speak, she saw how many people were crowded into the room and gasped. There were more than one hundred and forty people—I counted the names in the guest book after the service.

Afterwards, some people asked me if I regretted giving a kidney to someone who lived less than a year after the transplant (my mother, on hearing of Amelia's death, asked if I could get the kidney back). My "gift of life" had failed to save Amelia, after all. The implication of wasted sacrifice seemed to hang in the air in these conversations, but the implication was incorrect because no sacrifice was involved. I gave away something I did not need; I did not give Amelia my left arm, my right foot, or my cerebellum. But this is the kind of experiential body truth difficult to convey to anyone who has not donated a kidney—akin, perhaps, to describing sex or childbirth to someone who has never had these experiences. I have thought about the question of regret many times. The truth is that I had no expectation of a long life for Amelia, only the expectation that the Gauer kidney would improve her life by removing the need for dialysis. I cannot determine the precise number of days or months or years that should have accompanied this expectation.

In the end, the Frankenstein syndrome is a form of fantasy projection, from the healthy to the not-healthy. Our qualities, good or bad, do not reside in the organs in our bodies. Our qualities speak to our actions and our thoughts, our moral sense, our desires and dreams—not blood and tissue, or the nephrons of the kidney, or the stitching of a vein or artery. What we really seek to project through an organ donation is a fervent desire for the recipient to live and not die. So my answer is always no, I do not regret giving my left kidney to my granddaughter. Every night, when I undress, I see my body in the mirrored door of the wardrobe. I see the scar on the left side, just below the bottom rib, three inches long, the flesh still puckered and discoloured. The scar is both ugly and beautiful, a reminder of pain, but also a reminder of an action that was useful and generous. My body, myself.

And Inside, Silence
Sue Thomas

1

I spend a great deal of my time online, which means I sit down a
lot while my body does nothing much at all but type, think, and
shuffle around on an office chair. There was a time, when the World
Wide Web was young, when I and quite a few others lived the life
of the mind through the Internet and were so entranced by it that
we dared to hope the brain would transcend the body. Through the
power of virtuality and imagination we connected in the deepness
of cyberspace. Then, years before the noise and colour of places
such as Second Life, text-based virtual worlds such as LambdaMOO
drew us into deep silence. On those screens there were no pictures.
Words typed on a plain black screen represented your entire self. It
was there that I forgot my body and learned to be virtual, where the
most physical thing I ever did was put my hand against the glass at
a moment when someone else was doing the same on the other side
of the world, and our imaginations filled in the rest. Who needed
a body when the mind was exploding with intimacy? If you had
watched me then, you would have seen me seated and still for hours
at a time, only the hands moving, perhaps the eyes glancing back and
forth between the keyboard and the screen, and sometimes a smile,
a grimace, or even a tear. During that time my whole being would be
functioning only inside the machine, within which I experienced and
expressed emotion, curiosity, creativity, and rebellion.

Today my life online happens in other places, often on a phone
or laptop rather than a large static keyboard and monitor, but I'm

still inside cyberspace one way or another, and my mind still races ahead of my physical being. However, things have to change. The neglect has gone on too long, and now my body refuses to be ignored any further.

2

It's a slim glass bottle, about three inches tall, with a white label and gold-coloured screw-top. Inside it lie around a dozen small, light brown stones. I've never opened it until now, so when I unscrew the top I sniff at it somewhat nervously. This stuff was extracted from my gallbladder some ten years ago, and it could smell disgusting. But it doesn't. In fact, there is no smell at all. I shake the contents into the palm of my hand and roll them around with my fingers. They look like the kind of gravel you scatter around the base of houseplants. Variegated shades of light and dark tan, the largest the size of a small dried pea, the smallest like a mustard grain. Irregularly shaped but generally smooth. I push my thumbnail into one and break off a piece, then rub it hard until it crushes into golden chalky sand. For the purposes of research I should probably taste it, but the thought makes me nauseous, so I don't. I tip everything back into the bottle, screw on the cap, and go to wash my hands and scrub under my nails.

At the NASA Space Center in Houston I once touched a piece of moon rock, and holding these gallstones feels something like that: the same mysterious sense of contact with an alien object from very far away.

In his discussion of the phenomenology of viscera, philosopher Drew Leder points out that while the function of the "surface" body (skin, eyes, ears, etc.) is to collect and process external information, the smooth operation of the visceral organs depends upon them being protected and hidden, not just from view, but even from our awareness. When all is working well, we can't feel our viscera at all, and for the most part we forget they even exist. We're reminded of them only when there is a problem in the form of a locatable pain, such as the sharp agonies that had me crouching on the floor through many nights until my gallstones were finally removed, or a more generalized discomfort such as hunger, thirst, or the need to expel urine and feces. Medicine divides bodily sensations into three types: interoception (experienced by the internal body), exteroception (the five senses), and proprioception (balance, position, and muscular tension).

Leder draws our attention to the eating of an apple and how it is first examined, grasped, and eaten before being swallowed and entering the inner part of the body to be broken down and processed. Remnants of sensations, and even some sounds, may continue intermittently—reflux, indigestion, expellation—but "by far the greatest part of my vegetative processes lies submerged in impenetrable silence."

3

The gallstones were the first way my digestive system turned against me, and they were easily relieved by surgery. The second episode was much more long-term, indeed permanent. In 2007, my doctor became rather concerned because my weight was the highest it had ever been and I had been feeling increasingly miserable. The previous six months had been notable for various flare-ups of temper and anxiety, both at home and at work. That's not to say I am usually a sanguine person. I'm rather type A and tend to be led by enthusiasms and passions, throwing myself into a series of obsessions and working hard until I run out of steam. On the whole, though, I think I am fairly rational and on top of things. That, however, had started to change, as small issues that in the past would have demanded no more than a little extra attention began to really upset and preoccupy me. Food was the only thing that seemed to soothe my anxious exhaustion.

During long office afternoons, I grew more and more sleepy and would joke that my blood sugar was low and I needed coffee and cake to raise it again. In fact, as I was to find out, the problem was exactly the opposite. But it would take months before I really began to understand the mechanism of what was going on in my body, and even today I'm still not sure I really do.

As my weight rocketed as a result of attempting to simultaneously energize and calm myself with food, I went to my GP to beg for help in controlling my diet. He organized some tests. And so it was that I discovered I had developed type 2 diabetes. I was fifty-six. At the time of writing I've been living with type 2 for three years, and I'm still confused by it. There is indeed impenetrable silence—no pain, no discomfort, no loss of function—and yet I now have a serious and debilitating illness. How very strange.

4

When I was seventeen I worked for a while in the canteen of the Player's cigarette factory in Nottingham. My main jobs were buttering bread and washing up. At break-time we would sit around a table smoking free fags, drinking tea, and talking about sex. One of the girls was trying to get pregnant and anxious for advice on the best way to conceive, so she hung on to every word pronounced by an older woman who had six kids and was therefore an expert. What we needed to know, she told us, was that the womb is a sphere with one hole in it. Each month it goes through a full rotation and the best time to conceive is when the hole points downwards in alignment with the vagina.

"I'm sure that's not right!" I burst out. I'd read every book I could find on sexual reproduction, and I'd certainly never come across that one.

But my peers already didn't like me. It was clear from my manner and general demeanour that the Player's canteen was a stopgap job for me, whereas for most of the others it was a career choice. I was snobby, and now I claimed to know more about the workings of the human reproductive system than an experienced mother. They gave me the cold shoulder, and shortly afterwards I left for a job in an office, as they knew I would.

5

I thought about this incident when I started trying to understand diabetes, because I realized that my ignorance of my digestive processes was even worse than that of the woman who believed the womb rotated. I looked on the Web, of course, and discovered that diabetes was related to the pancreas. Although I had heard of this organ, I had no idea where it was, what it looked like, or which functions it performed. I poked around under my ribs but couldn't feel it. I'd been equally ignorant when I had gallstones, but at least they hurt like hell, so I had some rough idea of where they were lodged. But the pancreas doesn't feel like anything.

I watched some videos. *How the Body Works: Pancreas* sounds like all the biology classes I didn't pay attention to at school. The only thing I remember from five years of compulsory biology was the day when the teacher grabbed some coloured magic markers and a big piece of cardboard to sketch out a rough diagram of the digestive system, and Kevin, the cool ruffian of the class who always wore a studded leather jacket, fainted clean away. The teacher couldn't hide her smile as she helped him up from the floor. But this video doesn't make me feel dizzy. It's just sleep-inducing, with its pinky-grey illustrations and a narrator who was probably as bored by the whole thing as I was. I tried another—*Cirugía en un caso de pancreatitis*. Here is a real living pancreas, looking a bit like a large piece of blooded tripe. The patient is of course unconscious and mostly covered with operating theatre cloths. The voiceover is in Spanish; I'm not sure what the surgeon is doing, but she seems to be pulling the tripey stuff around as if preparing it for the dinner table. *Laparostomia per pancreatite acuta necrotico-emorragica* is a slideshow, but I can't tell what I'm looking at. Are those yellow things pieces of fat? They look like the custard-coloured pith of a pomegranate. And why does the organ appear to be wrapped up in a neatly folded parcel?

As I cruise from one surgery video to the next, I do start to feel genuinely repulsed. The inside of the body is so slippery and wet and complicated. So very red. How do we manage to keep all the bits in the right places inside our bags of waterproof skin? They look as if they should be constantly slithering around inside us, unanchored, so that you'd never know the location of your liver or your heart or your intestines from one minute to the next.

6

The week following my diabetes diagnosis I went back to the surgery for a long appointment to have it all explained to me. I took my daughter along as a second pair of ears in case I panicked and couldn't follow what the doctor said.

I would have to take a drug, Metformin, three times a day at mealtime. How long would it take, I asked, to cure the diabetes? He reminded me again that type 2 diabetes is a permanent and potentially degenerative condition that could involve insulin shots, and worse, farther down the line.

I've experienced very few illnesses in my life. Those I have had, like the gallstones, were treated with drugs or surgery until they went away. My close family is very fortunate to have suffered little illness, so I'm unfamiliar with disease and infirmity and have not had to deal with them very much at all. I have watched friends labouring to take care of aging parents, but first my father and then my mother died suddenly at the comparatively young age of sixty-three and sixty-nine. Dad had three heart attacks over several years. During the second one, he made it into the local newspaper when he suffered a coronary while driving and crashed his car at a roundabout. Nobody else was hurt, but Dad died and was revived three times on the way to hospital. He was hugely disappointed afterwards when he realized there had been no near-death experience or calls to walk toward the light. The third heart attack came while he was sitting at his desk at home doing paperwork and listening to country and western music. That one killed him instantly. As for Mom, she had high blood pressure for many years but was otherwise perfectly well. Then, several years after Dad died, she suffered a pulmonary embolism and passed away in the ambulance about an hour later on the way to hospital. Years before that, when I was nine, my grandmother died in her sleep of a stroke on one of the regular weekend nights that I shared her bed to keep her company and, presumably, give my mom a break from my restless presence at home. I woke up, assumed she was still asleep, and skipped back to my own house in the next street to have my breakfast.

So, in sum, I know very few people who have experienced serious debilitating illnesses. In my world, for the most part, the human body has followed a simple path of a few ups and downs curtailed by a sudden and simple final denouement.

7

The first recorded incidence of type 1 diabetes is documented in an Egyptian papyrus from 1550 BCE that refers to a disease that causes rapid weight loss and frequent urination. It was given the name *diabetes*, which means "a flowing through," by Greek physician Aretaeus somewhere between 60 and 90 CE. He also described it rather poetically as "the melting down of flesh and limbs into urine." (Type 2 diabetes involves very different symptoms and it was not identified until 1959.)

After Aretaeus, little is heard of diabetes until the Islamic Golden Age, when Persian philosopher and scientist Ibn Sīnā, sometimes called Avicenna (980–1037 CE) included it in his fourteen-volume *Canon of Medicine*. Then there was another gap of several hundred years until the Middle Ages, when it became usual practice for physicians to taste the urine of patients. That is when it was discovered that the urine of diabetes patients was often sweet—hence the addition of the word *mellitus* (honey) to the Latin name, *diabetes mellitus*.

8

I began my management routine. I learned how to use a special lance to prick my fingers and draw blood. I was really scared the first time I did it, afraid of the pain, but you soon learn the best way to do it as painlessly as possible and, really, it doesn't hurt. I'm certainly a lot better off than people who have to jab an insulin needle into their legs several times a day. After pricking my finger, I dip a test strip into the pearl of blood and then into a glucose meter to obtain a reading. At first I did this several times a day, before, after, and in between meals, to collect data on how my system was performing. Now I do it much less often. I take my tablets at the times prescribed, and I try somewhat pathetically and intermittently to lose weight. That of course had been my original aim when I first visited the doctor, and now it has become an imperative but one about which I am still frustratingly apathetic. And I'm pretty certain that too many hours spent surfing with my brain instead of my body is another contributing factor to my current condition. But to be honest—and I say this as one who has made a living from her experience of cyberspace and virtuality—the diabetes just doesn't feel real.

9

As Drew Leder points out in his popular study *The Absent Body*, the functions of the viscera are restricted and preordained. "Each organ plays its determined role, the lung in respiration, the stomach in food storage and breakdown . . . barring mishap, what reaches the lung will be air, the stomach, food or drink. Their fixed motile patterns will thus be adequate." In order for this to happen, the viscera must be protected from outside intervention and indeed from intervention by the owner of the body herself. I cannot make a decision not to digest the apple once I have swallowed it.

When you've been diagnosed with type 2, it's easy to fantasize about interoceptive sensations that may or may not be there. The glucose courses through my system invisibly and silently. If I feel weird or strangely out of sorts, it could be because my glucose is high or it could just be that I happen to feel weird that day. Nine times out of ten if I test when I feel weird, the reading is normal.

10

There are several kinds of diabetes: type 1 and type 2, plus the gestational diabetes that some women get during pregnancy, and perhaps even a type 3, currently the subject of research. Type 1 and type 2 are completely different from each other, and I've struggled to make sense of each of them. The following is—I think—what happens.

When you eat something, the glucose level in the blood rises and triggers the pancreas to produce insulin, which acts as a kind of key to open the doors to cells and let the glucose in. In type 1 diabetes, the pancreas does not make enough or stops making insulin, so the glucose can't be absorbed into the body, resulting in dangerously high levels, which can be corrected by injections of insulin. Without treatment, you can become hyperglycemic and go into shock.

In type 2, the pancreas functions normally, but the body is "insulin resistant" and doesn't allow the insulin to do its job. In contrast to type 1, which is about too little insulin resulting in high glucose levels, type 2 is about rising glucose levels. In this case, the pancreas responds by producing even more insulin in an effort to get the process working. That may help in the short term, but eventually the pancreas may no longer be able to produce enough insulin to keep glucose levels normal, and it may become necessary to take a drug, usually metformin hydrochloride, to artificially reduce them.

Sometimes the patient can avoid taking medication, or cease to need it, if she can lose enough weight to reduce stress on the pancreas. According to John Buse, president of the American Diabetes Association, most people with type 2 diabetes have the body of an SUV but the pancreas of a small sedan: "If they shrunk their frame, their pancreas would be just fine." I have to admit here and now in public that I have the body of a smallish SUV. Not an American SUV, admittedly, but certainly an English SUV. It would be good if I could get down to something like, say, a modestly sized hatchback.

Another transport metaphor I rather like is to imagine that the bloodstream contains little trains carrying glucose around the body to be off-loaded into the tissues wherever needed. In type 1, there is too much glucose in the little trains. In type 2 diabetes, the glucose is on board, but there is no way to off-load into the tissues. So the more glucose one takes in, the more it piles up inside the little trains, and the more starved of glucose the tissues become—but for a completely different reason than in type 1. So on those afternoons when I imagined I needed to "bump up my blood sugar" with a cake, what was really happening was that I already had quite enough sugar left over from lunch, but it wasn't reaching the places where it was needed. I was right to feel a lack, but I chose the wrong way to remedy it. On those occasions, too much sugar would make me not hypoglycemic, but hyperglycemic. Not too low, but too high, and hence the low functioning and sleepiness.

11

But even now that I understand my condition better, inside I still can't actually feel anything. When I look at my bottle of gallstones, I can imagine them swilling around in bile inside the gallbladder, and I can understand how they could obstruct a tube and cause acute pain. But when I pore over photos of pale-coloured meat and microscope images of the islets of Langerhans, or stare uncomprehendingly at the bloody videos made by surgeons for each other, I just have no sense of this entity, sometimes called "the hidden organ," which sits in the centre of my torso just above and behind my intestines.

Despite the SUVs and little trains, my pancreas remains a mystery. But why should that disturb me? It's not so very different from the years I spent in virtuality, dwelling for hours at a time inside a black-and-white screen. Today, much more serious things are happening, but I can't see or touch or hear or smell them. Inside, all is silence.

Acknowledgments and Further Reading

We would like to thank Ruth Linka and everyone at Brindle & Glass for their commitment to *In the Flesh*. One of the most rewarding aspects of assembling this book was reading for it, and we would like to share here some of the writing and imagery that fascinated, informed, and inspired us.

On the body and mind-body connection in general, we highly recommend *Body Shopping: Converting Body Parts to Profit* by Donna Dickenson (Oxford: Oneworld Publications, 2009); *The Kingdom of Infinite Space* by Raymond Tallis (Yale University Press, 2008); *Bodies* by Susie Orbach (New York: Picador, 2009); *The Body in Pain: The Making and Unmaking of the World* by Elaine Scarry (New York: Oxford University Press, 1985); *The Brain That Changes Itself* by Norman Doidge (New York: Penguin, 2007); *How Doctors Think* by Jerome Groopman (Boston/New York: Houghton Mifflin, 2007); *Leaves of Grass* by Walt Whitman (New York Modern Library, 1993); *Proust Was a Neuroscientist* by Jonah Lehrer (New York: Houghton Mifflin, 2007); *Carnal Knowledge: A Navel Gazer's Dictionary of Anatomy, Etymology, and Trivia* by Charles Hodgson (London: St. Martin's Press, 2007); *Becoming Animal: An Earthly Cosmology* by David Abram (New York: Pantheon Books, 2010), and, via Brian Brett, Robert Burton's eccentric and eclectic masterpiece *The Anatomy of Melancholy* (any unabridged edition) and *The Body: Photographs of the Human Form*, edited by William A. Ewing (London: Thames & Hudson, 1994).

Sue Thomas acknowledges the help of Dr. Anthony Nguyen and recommends *The Absent Body* by Drew Leder (London/Chicago: University of Chicago Press, 1990) and her own study, *Hello World: Travels in Virtuality* (York: Raw Nerve Press, 2004).

Regarding the face, Stenton Mackenzie's research page can be found at www.lifesci.dundee.ac.uk/projects/ftm-faces/FTM_faces/Welcome.html. Julian Gunn recommends *Body Alchemy: Transsexual Portraits* by Loren Cameron (California: Cleis Press, 1996) and *The Mind's Eye* by Oliver Sacks (New York: Knopf, 2010). Further reading could include *About Face* by Jonathan Cole (Massachusetts Institute of Technology Press, 1990); *Autobiography of a Face* by Lucy Grealy (New York: Houghton and Mifflin, 1994); and *The Story of My Face* (a novel) by Kathy Page (London: Weidenfeld & Nicolson, 2001.)

In connection with the ear, Margaret Thompson recommends *Journal of the Discovery of the Source of the Nile* by John Hanning Speke (first published in 1863) number 50 of the Everyman's Library (London, 1906).

As for the ever-busy hands, Kathy Page drew upon "The Anarchic Hand" by Sergio Della Sala in *The Psychologist* (journal of the British Psychological Society) 18:10; *The Hand: A Philosophical Enquiry into Human Being* by Raymond Tallis (Edinburgh University Press, 2003); *The Hand* by Frank R. Wilson (New York: Vintage, 1998); and *Saudi Arabi: A Secret State of Suffering*, Amnesty International Report, March 2000.

Concerning the womb and the breasts, respectively, Heather Kuttai and Lynne Van Luven refer to *Maternal Theory: Essential Readings* by Andrea O'Reilly (Toronto: Demeter Press, 2007) and *A History of the Breast* by Marilyn Yalom (New York: Knopf, 1997).

We would like to thank our wonderful contributors for joining us in this project, and to acknowledge each other: in this instance, two heads were a requirement and twenty fingers far more capable than ten.

Author Biographies

CAROLINE ADDERSON is the author of three novels (*A History of Forgetting, Sitting Practice, The Sky Is Falling*) and two collections of short stories (*Bad Imaginings, Pleased to Meet You*), as well as several books for young readers. Her work has received numerous prize nominations, including for the Scotiabank Giller Prize longlist, the Governor General's Literary Award, the Rogers' Trust Fiction Prize, and the Commonwealth Writers' Prize. A two-time Ethel Wilson Fiction Prize and three-time CBC Literary Award winner, Caroline was also the recipient of the 2006 Marian Engel Award for mid-career achievement.

ANDRÉ ALEXIS is a writer who lives in Toronto.

TAIAIAKE ALFRED was born in Montreal in 1964 and raised in the Mohawk community of Kahnawake. He was educated by Jesuits, served in the US Marine Corps infantry, and later earned degrees in history and political thought at Concordia University and Cornell University. His writings include scholarly books, opinion columns, personal essays, and humour. He is currently a professor at the University of Victoria and lives in the territory of the Wsanec Nation with his wife and three sons.

BRIAN BRETT is the author of eleven books of poetry, fiction, and memoir, including *Coyote: A Mystery, The Fungus Garden*, and *The Colour of Bones in a Stream*. He is a retired chair of the Writers' Union of Canada. His column in the *Yukon News*, "CultureWatch," ran for twelve years. Recently, he published two memoirs, *Uproar's Your Only Music* and *Trauma Farm*. His next memoir, *Tuco and the Scattershot World*, will complete this trilogy. He lives with his family on Salt Spring Island.

TREVOR COLE has written three novels. His most recent, *Practical Jean*, won the 2011 Leacock Medal for Humour and was shortlisted for the Writer's Trust Fiction Prize. His first two novels—*Norman Bray in the Performance of His Life* and *The Fearsome Particles*—were both shortlisted for the Governor General's Literary Award. And as one of Canada's leading magazine journalists, Trevor has won nine National Magazine Awards, including three gold medals. He currently lives in Hamilton, Ontario.

A former professional ballet dancer and choreographer, DEDE CRANE is the author of the nationally acclaimed novel *Sympathy*, a collection of stories, *The Cult of Quick Repair*, and two novels for teens. She is the co-editor, along with Lisa Moore, of a book of essays on birth titled *Great Expectations*. She teaches in the writing department at the University of Victoria.

LORNA CROZIER'S latest books are the memoir *Small Beneath the Sky*, which won the Hubert Evans Award for Nonfiction, and the book of poetry *Small Mechanics*. A distinguished professor at the University of Victoria, she is the recipient of several awards, including the Governor General's Award, and two honorary doctorates for her contributions to Canadian literature. She has read her poetry at literary festivals around the world. She lives on Vancouver Island with poet Patrick Lane and two fine cats.

CANDACE FERTILE has a PHD in English from the University of Alberta, teaches at Camosun College in Victoria, BC, and would rather read than do anything else. Sleeping, writing, and travelling are tied for second place. She reviews books for a number of Canadian publications and is a member of the editorial collective of *Room*, Canada's oldest literary magazine of women's writing.

STEPHEN GAUER's prize-winning short stories have been published in *Descant, Prairie Fire*, the *Toronto Star*, and *Best Canadian Stories 10* (Oberon Press). His novel *Hold Me Now* was published in 2011.

By the time you read this, JULIAN GUNN will hopefully have completed his master's degree at the University of Victoria. His personal nonfiction is also included in the TouchWood anthology *Nobody's Father*. He appears at this juncture to be in some danger of writing a memoir. His friend Stenton Mackenzie is in Scotland for the immediate future, to everyone else's envy.

A public speaker, leader, activist, administrator, coach, athlete, writer, and mother, HEATHER KUTTAI has been spinal cord injured and a wheelchair user for more than three decades. In 2010, she wrote, published, and went on a national tour with her first book, *Maternity Rolls: Pregnancy, Childbirth, and Disability*. The book was shortlisted for a Saskatchewan Book Award. She has been married to her high-school sweetheart, Darrell Seib, for twenty-one years, and they have two children, Patrick and Chelsea.

LYNNE VAN LUVEN has taught writing, with an emphasis on creative nonfiction, at the University of Victoria since 1997. She has a PHD in Canadian literature from the University of Alberta and has been a journalist and editor for a good part of her working life. She has edited or co-edited five previous books of nonfiction, including *Going Some Place, Nobody's Mother, Nobody's Father*, and *Somebody's Child: Stories About Adoption*, published in 2011. She believes the personal essay is one of the most important forms of nonfiction expression and also applauds the memoirists who struggle toward narrative honesty.

SUSAN OLDING's first book, *Pathologies: A Life in Essays*, won the 2010 Creative Nonfiction Collective's Readers' Choice Award and was longlisted for the BC National Award for Canadian Nonfiction. Her work has been widely anthologized and she is the recipient of several prizes and awards, including the Edna Award from *The New Quarterly* and the Brenda Ueland Prose Prize for Literary Nonfiction (US). She lives in Kingston, Ontario.

KATHY PAGE has worked as a carpenter and as a painter, and still enjoys manual labour. Her seven novels include *The Story of My Face*, longlisted for the Orange Prize in 2002; *Alphabet*, shortlisted for a Governor General's Award in 2005; and *The Find*, shortlisted for the 2011 ReLit Novel Award. She is also a winner of the Bridport International Prize for short fiction and the Traveller Award, and a contributor to many prose anthologies. She moved with her family from London, England, to Salt Spring Island in 2001. Find her at www.KathyPage.info.

KATE PULLINGER'S most recent novel, *The Mistress of Nothing*, won the Governor General's Award for Fiction in 2009. She is the author of many books and works of digital fiction, including the multi-award-winning *Inanimate Alice*. She was born in the Rockies, went to high school outside Victoria, and lives in London, England. Find her at www.katepullinger.com.

MERILYN SIMONDS is the author of fifteen books, including the Canadian creative nonfiction classic *The Convict Lover*, nominated for a Governor General's Award. Her short stories are published internationally, and her novel *The Holding* was selected as a *New York Times Book Review* Editor's Choice. With Wayne Grady, she co-authored *Breakfast at the Exit Café: Travels in America*. Her most recent book is *A New Leaf: Growing with My Garden*, a collection of personal essays rooted in her gardens near Kingston, Ontario.

RICHARD STEEL has lived in British Columbia since 2001 and is the father of two children and the husband of one wife. This is his first piece of writing in seventeen years and his first published work in Canada. He is a woodworker, furniture maker, and coach of youth soccer. He has driven a 1953 London double-decker bus around the world and has worked on oil rigs in Alberta and in interior design shops in London. He is blessed with a sense of humour and the hope that he will once again, and soon, be able to move without pain.

MADELEINE THIEN is the author of three books of fiction, including her most recent novel, *Dogs at the Perimeter*. Her fiction and essays have appeared in *Granta*, *The Walrus*, *Five Dials*, *Brick*, and the *Asia Literary Review*, and her work has been translated into more than sixteen languages. In 2010, she received the Ovid Festival Prize, awarded each year to an international writer of promise. She lives in Montreal.

SUE THOMAS writes about the Internet and social media. Her last book, *Hello World: Travels in Virtuality* (2004), is a travelogue of life online, and she is currently writing *Nature and Cyberspace: Stories, Memes and Metaphors*. Her first novel, the cybernetic romance *Correspondence*, was shortlisted for the 1992 Arthur C. Clarke Award. She is a professor of new media at De Montfort University, Leicester, England. Follow her on Twitter @suethomas or visit her website at suethomas.net.

MARGARET THOMPSON came to Canada from England in 1967 and taught English at secondary and postsecondary institutions for many years until her retirement in 1998. She is the author of six books, including two collections of personal essays, the most recent being *Adrift on the Ark: Our Connection to the Natural World* (Brindle & Glass, 2009). She is a past president of the Federation of BC Writers. She now lives in Victoria, BC.